I Wish *I'd* Said That

EDITED BY

NED SHERRIN

OXFORD

UNIVERSITY PRESS

OXFORD

UNIVERSITY PRESS

Great Clarendon Street, Oxford OX2 6DP

Oxford University Press is a department of the University of Oxford.
It furthers the University's objective of excellence in research, scholarship,
and education by publishing worldwide in

Oxford New York

Athens Auckland Bangkok Bogotá Buenos Aires Cape Town
Chennai Dar es Salaam Delhi Florence Hong Kong Istanbul Karachi
Kolkata Kuala Lumpur Madrid Melbourne Mexico City Mumbai Nairobi
Paris São Paulo Shanghai Singapore Taipei Tokyo Toronto Warsaw

with associated companies in Berlin Ibadan

British Library Cataloguing in Publication Data

Data available

Library of Congress Cataloging in Publication Data

I wish I'd said that / edited by Ned Sherrin.
p. cm.
1. Quotations, English. I. Title: I wish I had said that. II. Sherrin, Ned
PN6081.I18 2004
082–dc22 2004056804

ISBN 0–19–860988–4

10 9 8 7 6 5 4 3 2 1

Designed by Paul Saunders
Typeset in ITC Stone Serif and Stone
by Interactive Sciences Ltd
Printed in Great Britain by
Biddles Ltd

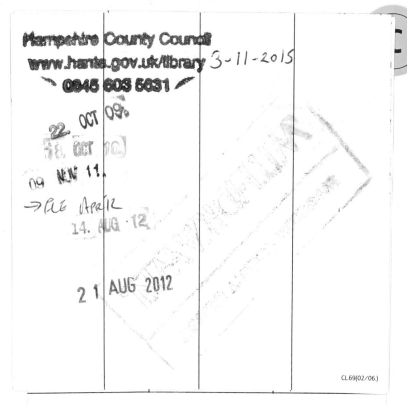

Hampshire
County Council

∠IT

Please return/renew this item
by the last date shown.
Books may also be renewed by
phone or the Internet.

**Hampshire County Council
Library & Information Service**

http://libcat.hants.gov.uk

Contents

Preface

A quotation is often a conversational lifeline—here it supplies a title. The immediate source is Oscar Wilde. In a rare appearance as a 'straight man', he complimented James Whistler on a quip with the words, 'I wish I'd said that.' Whistler devastatingly replied, 'You will, Oscar, you will.'

Bitter is the regret when one fails to get the last telling word: worse is the feeling when it comes to one, but comes too late. In the 18th century Diderot, in *Paradoxe sur le Comédien*, identified this predicament as '*l'esprit de l'escalier*' or 'staircase wit', the cutting reply one thinks of only when one has left the drawing room and is already on the way downstairs. Many years ago, to my great delight, I coined the phrase, 'Repartee is what one thinks of on the way home.' Deluded, I thought that I got there first.

The sources quoted in this book alone know how many of the remarks collected here were new minted, recollected in humiliation halfway down *l'escalier*, reworked, recycled, or simply stolen. Gore Vidal scored a palpable hit on a Radio 4 programme in the 1970s when Richard Adams dismissed his novel *Lincoln* as 'meretricious'. Vidal responded swiftly with, 'Really? Well, meretricious and a happy New Year to you too!' Laughter around the *Start the Week* table took no account of earlier citings of this response attributed to Franklin P. Adams in America in the early 1930s and on the NBC radio shows starring the Marx Brothers, *Flywheel, Shyster and Flywheel*, in 1933.

The criteria for selection are bound to be subjective. Everyone has his or her own idea of what is funny. Molière's test was immediacy, 'The true touchstone of wit is the impromptu.' So, some remarks are fired from the hip. La Rochefoucauld saw a social advantage, 'Wit enables us to act rudely with impunity.' (If you are lucky.) But La Rochefoucauld did not intrinsically value wit, 'If it were not for the company of fools, a witty man would often be greatly at a loss.' Wycherley, on the other hand, thought wit 'more necessary than beauty: and I think no young woman ugly who has it and no handsome woman agreeable without it'. Congreve demanded a level playing field, 'Wit must be foiled by wit: cut a diamond with a diamond.'

Humour admits the possibility of good nature. Does wit? While Addison thought, 'the greatest wits I have conversed with are men eminent for their humanity', Sheridan took the opposite view, 'There is no possibility of being witty without a little ill-nature.' For a wit, Sydney Smith was sceptical. 'Professed wits, though they are generally courted for the amusement they afford, are seldom respected for the qualities they possess.' Benjamin Franklin lines up with Smith. 'There's many witty men whose brains can't fill their bellies.' So does Hazlitt: 'Those who cannot miss an opportunity of saying a good thing...are not to be trusted with the management of any great question.'

Nevertheless we welcome them and we would not have this book without them—some famous, some obscure, and some who cause us to smile inadvertently.

Dorothy Parker's name, like those of Wilde, Shaw, Twain, Coward, Waugh, and a dozen others, creates a sense of anticipation with the phrase 'as Dorothy Parker said...' Indeed, Parker's quotability got her into a Cole Porter lyric:

As Dorothy Parker once said to her boyfriend,
'Fare thee well.'
As Columbus announced when he knew he was bounced,
'It was swell, Isabelle, swell.'...

It was just one of those things.

For Dorothy Parker truth was an important factor. 'Truth is important. There is a hell of a difference between wisecracking and wit. Wit has truth in it. Wisecracking is simply callisthenics with words.' I daresay a few wisecracks have slipped in.

Restrictions of space make for some regretted omissions. Although we admit Dorothy Parker's notorious verdict on the acting of Katharine Hepburn in *The Lake* in 1933, 'She ran the whole gamut of the emotions from A to B,' there is no room for the lethal sentence in which she went on to refer to the fine supporting actress Alison Skipworth, 'Miss Hepburn kept well upstage of Miss Skipworth, *lest she catch acting from her.*' Many

splendid one-liners, of course, represent the climax of an anec-
dote for which the preparatory story would be required.

As an inveterate clipper of newspapers I have culled many of
the more recent quotations from the papers. So Edwina Currie's
comment on John Major's autobiography, 'I wasn't even in the
index!' rubs shoulders with Lytton Strachey's classic, 'Discretion
is not the better part of biography.' And in the section devoted to
The Body, Dolly Parton's 'If I see something sagging, dragging or
bagging, I get it sucked, tucked or plucked,' can cohabit with
Cyril Connolly's venerable 'Imprisoned in every fat man a thin
one is wildly signalling to be let out.'

As this Preface goes to press more examples turn up. This one
will have to wait to find a place in the third edition of the *Oxford
Dictionary of Humorous Quotations*. In Christopher Robbins's biography of the film director Brian Desmond Hurst, *The Empress
of Ireland*, he records Desmond Hurst's boast that he was tri-
sexual: 'The Army, the Navy and the Household Cavalry.' Of the
collecting of many quips, like the making of many books, there
is happily no end.

May 2004

NED SHERRIN

List of Subjects

Acting

> 66 Acting is merely the art of keeping a large group of people from coughing. 99
>
> **RALPH RICHARDSON**

supposed advice to a young actor:
Try and look as if you had a younger brother in Shropshire.
J. M. Barrie

I'm out of a job. London wants flappers, and I can't flap.
Mrs Patrick Campbell, *of the theatre of 1927*

When I read 'Be real, don't get caught acting,' I thought, 'How the hell do you do that?'
Billy Connolly

CLAUDETTE COLBERT: I knew these lines backwards last night.
NOËL COWARD: And that's just the way you're saying them this morning.
Noël Coward

Dear Ingrid—speaks five languages and can't act in any of them.

John Gielgud, *of Ingrid Bergman*

Shakespeare is so tiring. You never get a chance to sit down unless you're a king.

Josephine Hull

I have worked with more submarines than leading ladies.

John Mills

When you do Shakespeare they think you must be intelligent because they *think* you understand what you're saying.

Helen Mirren

of Katherine Hepburn at the first night of The Lake *(1933)*
She ran the whole gamut of the emotions from A to B.

Dorothy Parker

Working with her was like being hit over the head with a Valentine's Day card.

Christopher Plummer, *of Julie Andrews*

They say an actor is only as good as his parts. Well, my parts have done me pretty well, darling.

Barbara Windsor

Advertising

> **66** Advertising is the rattling of a stick inside a swill bucket. **99**
>
> **GEORGE ORWELL**

Advertising is the most fun you can have with your clothes on.

Jerry Della Femina

Society drives people crazy with lust and calls it advertising.

John Lahr

Advertising may be described as the science of arresting human intelligence long enough to get money from it.

Stephen Leacock

The consumer isn't a moron; she is your wife.

David Ogilvy

Anger

> 66 It is never difficult to distinguish between a Scotsman with a grievance and a ray of sunshine. 99
>
> **P. G. WODEHOUSE**

Anger makes dull men witty, but it keeps them poor.
Francis Bacon

D'oh!
Matt Groening, *Homer Simpson's habitual expression of annoyance*

Don't have a cow, man!
Matt Groening, *Bart Simpson's response to anger*

I left the room with silent dignity, but caught my foot in the mat.
George Grossmith and Weedon Grossmith

It's my rule never to lose me temper till it would be dethrimental to keep it.
Sean O'Casey

When angry, count four; when very angry, swear.
Mark Twain

Ice formed on the butler's upper slopes.
P. G. Wodehouse

He spoke with a certain what-is-it in his voice, and I could see that, if not actually disgruntled, he was far from being gruntled.
P. G. Wodehouse

Appearance

> 66 I always say beauty is only sin deep. 99
>
> SAKI

My face looks like a wedding cake left out in the rain.
W. H. Auden

It often means vanity and sometimes drink.
Lord Baden-Powell, *explaining his mistrust of 'men with waxed moustaches'*

I know I looked awful because my mother phoned and said I looked lovely.

Jo Brand, *after getting a makeover on television*

Glamour is on a life-support machine and not expected to live.

Joan Collins

I guess a drag queen's like an oil painting: You gotta stand back from it to get the full effect.

Harvey Fierstein

I do not think if I had had a full head of hair, there would have been a Tory landslide.

William Hague

I kept thinking, if his face was that wrinkled, what did his balls look like?

David Hockney, *after drawing W. H. Auden*

Such cruel glasses.

Frankie Howerd, *of Robin Day*

RICHARD: You look fabulous!
ALLY MCBEAL: I know, I just got fired for it.

David E. Kelley

In Los Angeles everyone has perfect teeth. It's crocodile land.

Gwyneth Paltrow

If beauty is truth, why don't women go to the library to have their hair done?

Lily Tomlin

By the time you hit 50, I reckon you've earned your wrinkles, so why not be proud of them?

Twiggy

I was so ugly when I was born, the doctor slapped my mother.

Henny Youngman

Argument

> 66 I'll not listen to reason...Reason always means what someone else has got to say. 99
>
> **ELIZABETH GASKELL**

Sir Roger told them, with the air of a man who would not give his judgement rashly, that much might be said on both sides.

Joseph Addison

You can't turn a thing upside down if there's no theory about it being the right way up.

G. K. Chesterton

'My idea of an agreeable person,' said Hugo Bohun, 'is a person who agrees with me.'

Benjamin Disraeli

Any stigma, as the old saying is, will serve to beat a dogma.

Philip Guedalla

Several excuses are always less convincing than one.
Aldous Huxley

I think it will be a clash between the political will and the administrative won't.
Jonathan Lynn and Antony Jay

And who are you? said he.—Don't puzzle me, said I.
Laurence Sterne

When two strong men stand face to face, each claiming to be Major Brabazon-Plank, it is inevitable that there will be a sense of strain, resulting in a momentary silence.
P. G. Wodehouse

Art

> It's amazing what you can do with an E in A-level art, twisted imagination and a chainsaw
>
> **DAMIEN HIRST**

If a scientist were to cut his ear off, no one would take it as evidence of a heightened sensibility.

Peter Medawar

A lot of being an artist is sitting around in an underheated room with Radio 4 on, chipping away.

Grayson Perry

My art belongs to Dada.

Cole Porter

If you want art to be like ovaltine, then clearly some art is not for you.

Peter Reading

I don't know what art is, but I do know what it isn't. And it isn't someone walking around with a salmon over his shoulder, or embroidering the name of everyone they have slept with on the inside of a tent.

Brian Sewell

Painters are so bitchy. Magritte told Miró that Kandinsky had feet of Klee.

Dick Vosburgh

in his case against Ruskin, replying to the question: 'For two days' labour, you ask two hundred guineas?':
No, I ask it for the knowledge of a lifetime.

James McNeill Whistler

 **Awards**

 Awards are like piles. Sooner or later, every bum gets one.

MAUREEN LIPMAN

Prizes are like sashes, you can wear them and be Miss World for a bit...I've been royally dissed by prizes.

Martin Amis

My career must be slipping. This is the first time I've been available to pick up an award.
Michael Caine

Oscar night at my house is called Passover.
Bob Hope

The cross of the Legion of Honour has been conferred upon me. However, few escape that distinction.
Mark Twain

People fail you, children disappoint you, thieves break in, moths corrupt, but an OBE goes on for ever.
Fay Weldon

Behaviour

> **66** Manners are especially the need of the plain. The pretty can get away with anything. **99**
>
> **EVELYN WAUGH**

You know what charm is: a way of getting the answer yes without having asked any clear question.
   Albert Camus

Curtsey while you're thinking what to say. It saves time.
   Lewis Carroll

I always take blushing either for a sign of guilt, or of ill breeding.
   William Congreve

Suspect all extraordinary and groundless civilities.
   Thomas Fuller

I have noticed that the people who are late are often so much jollier than the people who have to wait for them.
   E. V. Lucas

Good manners are a combination of intelligence, education, taste, and style mixed together so that you don't need any of those things.

P. J. O'Rourke

Do you suppose I could buy back my introduction to you?

S. J. Perelman et al.

One of those telegrams of which M. de Guermantes had wittily fixed the formula: 'Cannot come, lie follows'.

Marcel Proust

This is a free country, madam. We have a right to share your privacy in a public place.

Peter Ustinov

It is a good rule in life never to apologize. The right sort of people do not want apologies, and the wrong sort take a mean advantage of them.

P. G. Wodehouse

Biography

 Discretion is not the better part of biography. 99

LYTTON STRACHEY

Biography should be written by an acute enemy.
Arthur James Balfour

An autobiography is an obituary in serial form with the last instalment missing.
Quentin Crisp

I wasn't even in the index.
Edwina Currie, *on John Major's autobiography*

Autobiography is now as common as adultery and hardly less reprehensible.
John Grigg

To write one's memoirs is to speak ill of everybody except oneself.
Henri Philippe Pétain

Biography is the mesh through which real life escapes.
Tom Stoppard

I have a good track record with larger-than-life iron ladies.
Carol Thatcher, *on writing the story of the liner QEII*

Only when one has lost all curiosity about the future has one reached the age to write an autobiography.
Evelyn Waugh

Then there is my noble and biographical friend who has added a new terror to death.
Charles Wetherell, *on Lord Campbell's* Lives of the Lord Chancellors *being written without the consent of heirs or executors*

Every great man nowadays has his disciples, and it is always Judas who writes the biography.
Oscar Wilde

The Body

> 66 Imprisoned in every fat man a thin one is wildly signalling to be let out. 99
>
> CYRIL CONNOLLY

People don't come in my size until they're old...I used to think people were born with big bones and large frames, but apparently these grow when you're about sixty-eight.

Maeve Binchy

I'm tired of all this nonsense about beauty being only skin-deep. That's deep enough. What do you want—an adorable pancreas?

Jean Kerr

If I see something sagging, dragging or bagging I get it sucked, tucked or plucked.

Dolly Parton

I'm deeply honoured, but a bit confused. I was only ever a B-cup.

Diana Rigg, *on being voted the sexiest television star 'of all time' by Americans*

I don't really like knees.
Yves Saint Laurent

It's hard to be naked and not be upstaged by your nipples.
Susan Sarandon

The body of a young woman is God's greatest achievement...Of course, He could have built it to last longer but you can't have everything.
Neil Simon

She had very thick ankles.
Thomas Griffiths Wainewright, *his justification for poisoning his sister-in-law*

Let's forget the six feet and talk about the seven inches.
Mae West

Free your mind, and your bottom will follow.
Duchess of York, *slimming advice*

Books

 Book—what they make a movie out of for television.

LEONARD LOUIS LEVINSON

The world may be full of fourth-rate writers but it's also full of fourth-rate readers.

Stan Barstow

I read part of it all the way through.

Sam Goldwyn

Having been unpopular in high school is not just cause for book publication.

Fran Lebowitz

This is not a novel to be tossed aside lightly. It should be thrown with great force.

Dorothy Parker

I have known her pass the whole evening without mentioning a single book, or *in fact anything unpleasant,* at all.

Henry Reed

I hate books; they only teach us to talk about things we know nothing about.

Jean-Jacques Rousseau

I like to have exciting evenings on holiday, because after you've spent 8 hours reading on the beach you don't feel like turning in early with a good book.

Arthur Smith

A best-seller is the gilded tomb of a mediocre talent.

Logan Pearsall Smith

No furniture so charming as books.

Sydney Smith

'*Classic.*' A book which people praise and don't read.

Mark Twain

I haven't been so happy since the day Reader's Digest lost my address.

Dick Vosburgh

Bores

 A person who talks when you wish him
to listen.

AMBROSE BIERCE

What's wrong with being a boring kind of guy?
George Bush

He is not only dull in himself, but the cause of dullness in others.
Samuel Foote, *on a dull law lord*

A bore is simply a nonentity who resents his humble lot in life, and seeks satisfaction for his wounded ego by forcing himself on his betters.
H. L. Mencken

He was not only a bore; he bored for England.
Malcolm Muggeridge, *of Anthony Eden*

A bore is a man who, when you ask him how he is, tells you.
Bert Leston Taylor

Dylan talked copiously, then stopped. 'Somebody's boring me,' he said, 'I think it's me.'
   Dylan Thomas

Only dull people are brilliant at breakfast.
   Oscar Wilde

Boxing

> 66 The bigger they are, the further they have to fall. 99
>
>   **ROBERT FITZSIMMONS**

Boxing is show-business with blood.
   David Belasco, *later also used by Frank Bruno*

And I want to say anything is possible. Comma. You know.
   Frank Bruno

Tall men come down to my height when I hit 'em in the body.
   Jack Dempsey

after Jack Sharkey beat Max Schmeling (of whom Jacobs was manager) in the heavyweight title fight, 21 June 1932:
We was robbed!
    Joe Jacobs

I miss the things like the cameraderie in the gym. I don't miss being smacked in the mouth every day.
    Barry McGuigan, *on retirement from the ring*

Bureaucracy

> Perfection of planned layout is achieved only by institutions on the point of collapse.
>
> **C. NORTHCOTE PARKINSON**

A memorandum is written not to inform the reader but to protect the writer.
    Dean Acheson

I confidently expect that we [civil servants] shall continue to be grouped with mothers-in-law and Wigan Pier as one of the recognized objects of ridicule.
    Edward Bridges

The Pentagon, that immense monument to modern man's subservience to the desk.
   Oliver Franks

his secretary had suggested throwing away out-of-date files:
A good idea, only be sure to make a copy of everything before getting rid of it.
   Sam Goldwyn

A civil servant doesn't make jokes.
   Eugène Ionesco

on his dislike of working in teams:
A camel is a horse designed by a committee.
   Alec Issigonis

By the time the civil service has finished drafting a document to give effect to a principle, there may be little of the principle left.
   Lord Reith

Business

 The public be damned! I'm working for my stockholders. 99

WILLIAM H. VANDERBILT

Our clients are coping with the stress of financial loss by soaking in a hot bath scented with my Rose Geranium bath crystals.

Elizabeth Arden, *on the Wall Street crash*

My first rule of consumerism is never to buy anything you can't make your children carry.

Bill Bryson

When people ask me whether I'd rather be thought of as a funny man or a great boss, my answer is always the same: they are not mutually exclusive.

Ricky Gervais and Stephen Merchant, *David Brent as manager*

Only the paranoid survive.

Andrew Grove

Accountants are the witch-doctors of the modern world
and willing to turn their hands to any kind of magic.
  Lord Justice Harman

The last stage of fitting the product to the market is fitting
the market to the product.
  Clive James

We even sell a pair of earrings for under £1, which is
cheaper than a prawn sandwich from Marks & Spencers.
But I have to say the earrings probably won't last as long.
  Gerald Ratner

Running a company on market research is like driving
while looking in the rear view mirror.
  Anita Roddick

Whenever I feel in the least tempted to be methodical or
business-like or even decently industrious, I go to Kensal
Green and look at the graves of those who died in business.
  Saki

I long for the day when a new generation of Anita Roddicks
can address the AGM in a bright pink dress and strappy
sandals.
  Alexandra Shulman

Put all your eggs in one basket—and WATCH THAT BASKET.
  Mark Twain

Lunch is for wimps.
Stanley Weiser and Oliver Stone

Nothing is illegal if one hundred well-placed business men decide to do it.
Andrew Young

Censorship

66 I'm all in favour of free expression provided it's kept rigidly under control. 99

ALAN BENNETT

Everybody favours free speech in the slack moments when no axes are being ground.
Heywood Broun

I dislike censorship. Like an appendix it is useless when inert and dangerous when active.
Maurice Edelman

No government ought to be without censors: and where the press is free, no one ever will.

Thomas Jefferson

Freedom of the press is guaranteed only to those who own one.

A. J. Liebling

Censorship, like charity, should begin at home, but, unlike charity, it should end there.

Clare Boothe Luce

A censor is a man who knows more than he thinks you ought to.

Laurence J. Peter

Assassination is the extreme form of censorship.

George Bernard Shaw

Certainty

> 66 I'll give you a definite maybe. 99
>
> **SAM GOLDWYN**

He used to be fairly indecisive, but now he's not so certain.
Peter Alliss

You can put up a sign on the door, 'beware of the dog',
without having a dog.
Hans Blix

We can dance on pinheads till the cows come home.
Alastair Campbell

I don't believe in astrology; I'm a Sagittarius and we're
sceptical.
Arthur C. Clarke

I wish I was as cocksure of anything as Tom Macaulay is of
everything.
Lord Melbourne

That happy sense of purpose people have when they are standing up for a principle they haven't really been knocked down for yet.

P. J. O'Rourke

Ohhh, I don't *believe* it!

David Renwick, *Victor Meldrew's catchphrase*

All right, have it your own way—you heard a seal bark!

James Thurber

 **Character**

66 I've met a lot of hardboiled eggs in my time, but you're twenty minutes. 99

BILLY WILDER

Take care not to be the kind of person for whom the band is always playing in the other room.

Quentin Crisp

Claudia's the sort of person who goes through life holding on to the sides.

Alice Thomas Ellis

He's so wet you could shoot snipe off him.
   Anthony Powell

She was the sort of woman who, if she had been taken in adultery, would have caught the first stone and thrown it back.
   Anthony Powell

You can tell a lot about a fellow's character by his way of eating jellybeans.
   Ronald Reagan

Felix? Playing around? Are you crazy? He wears a vest and galoshes.
   Neil Simon

I am afraid that he has one of those terribly weak natures that are not susceptible to influence.
   Oscar Wilde

Slice him where you like, a hellhound is always a hellhound.
   P. G. Wodehouse

Children

 There never was a child so lovely but his mother was glad to get asleep.

RALPH WALDO EMERSON

The place is very well and quiet and the children only scream in a low voice.

Lord Byron

I'll thcream and thcream and thcream till I'm thick. And I *can.*

Richmal Crompton, *Violet Elizabeth Bott's habitual threat*

It's like hanging out with two miniature drunks.

Johnny Depp, *on his children*

at the first night of J. M. Barrie's Peter Pan*:*
Oh, for an hour of Herod!

Anthony Hope

definition of a baby:
A loud noise at one end and no sense of responsibility at the other.
  Ronald Knox

Ask your child what he wants for dinner only if he's buying.
  Fran Lebowitz

Anybody can have one kid. But going from one kid to two is like going from owning a dog to running a zoo.
  P. J. O'Rourke

All bachelors love dogs, and we would love children just as much if they could be taught to retrieve.
  P. J. O'Rourke

Children are given us to discourage our better emotions.
  Saki

Childhood is Last Chance Gulch for happiness. After that, you know too much.
  Tom Stoppard

Children begin by loving their parents; after a time they judge them; rarely, if ever, do they forgive them.
  Oscar Wilde

Choice

> He had polyester sheets and I wanted to get cotton sheets. He discussed it with his shrink many times before he made the switch.
>
> **MIA FARROW**

I'll have what she's having.

Nora Ephron, *woman to waiter, seeing Sally acting an orgasm*

asked which film he would like to see while convalescing:
Anything except that damned Mouse.

George V

'You oughtn't to yield to temptation.' 'Well, somebody must, or the thing becomes absurd,' said I.

Anthony Hope

Too rich and you lose sight of reality; too thin and you end up dead.

Shazia Mirza

A compromise in the sense that being bitten in half by a shark is a compromise with being swallowed whole.

P. J. O'Rourke

in the post office, pointing at the centre of a sheet of stamps:
I'll take that one.

Herbert Beerbohm Tree

Christmas

> 66 A Merry Christmas to all my friends except two. 99
>
> W. C. FIELDS

I have often thought, says Sir Roger, it happens very well that Christmas should fall out in the Middle of Winter.

Joseph Addison

Cancel the kitchen scraps for lepers and orphans. No more merciful beheadings. And call off Christmas!

Pen Densham and John Watson, *the Sheriff of Nottingham in festive mood*

I am a poor man, but I would gladly give ten shillings to find out who sent me the insulting Christmas card I received this morning.

George Grossmith and Weedon Grossmith

FIORELLO (Chico Marx): You can't fool me. There ain't no Sanity Claus.

George S. Kaufman and Morrie Ryskind

Christmas begins about the first of December with an office party and ends when you finally realize what you spent, around April fifteenth of the next year.

P. J. O'Rourke

Christmas, that time of year when people descend into the bunker of the family.

Byron Rogers

It will be a very traditional Christmas, with presents, crackers, doors slamming and people bursting into tears, but without the big dead thing in the middle.

Victoria Wood, *of a vegetarian Christmas*

The Cinema

66 Pictures are for entertainment, messages should be delivered by Western Union. 99

SAM GOLDWYN

There are no rules in filmmaking. Only sins. And the cardinal sin is dullness.

Frank Capra

Our comedies are not to be laughed at.

Sam Goldwyn

That's the way with these directors, they're always biting the hand that lays the golden egg.

Sam Goldwyn

What we need is a story that starts with an earthquake and works its way up to a climax.

Sam Goldwyn

The trouble with this business is that the stars keep 90% of the money.

Lew Grade

If I made *Cinderella*, the audience would immediately be looking for a body in the coach.

Alfred Hitchcock

Porn? That's films where the plot doesn't thicken.

Sean Lock

Hollywood money isn't money. It's congealed snow, melts in your hand, and there you are.

Dorothy Parker

Once a month the sky falls on my head, I come to, and I see another movie I want to make.

Steven Spielberg

I like the old masters, by which I mean John Ford, John Ford, and John Ford.

Orson Welles

The first nine commandments for a director are 'Thou shalt not bore.' The tenth is 'Thou shalt have the right of final cut.'

Billy Wilder

Class

> 66 Just because I have made a point of never losing my accent it doesn't mean I am an eel-and-pie yob. 99
>
> **MICHAEL CAINE**

I am not quite a gentleman but you would hardly notice it but can't be helped anyhow.

Daisy Ashford

His lordship may compel us to be equal upstairs, but there will never be equality in the servants' hall.

J. M. Barrie

Mankind is divisible into two great classes: hosts and guests.

Max Beerbohm

Accent is the snake and the ladder in the upstairs downstairs of social ambition.

Melvyn Bragg

A branch of one of your antediluvian families, fellows that the flood could not wash away.
William Congreve

Gentlemen do not take soup at luncheon.
Lord Curzon

We are all Adam's children but silk makes the difference.
Thomas Fuller

When I want a peerage, I shall buy it like an honest man.
Lord Northcliffe

'She's leaving her present house and going to Lower Seymour Street.' 'I dare say she will, if she stays there long enough.'
Saki

I don't want to talk grammar, I want to talk like a lady.
George Bernard Shaw

The English country gentleman galloping after a fox—the unspeakable in full pursuit of the uneatable.
Oscar Wilde

Colours

> 66 I cannot pretend to feel impartial about the colours. I rejoice with the brilliant ones, and am genuinely sorry for the poor browns. 99
>
> **WINSTON CHURCHILL**

Gentlemen never wear brown in London.
  Lord Curzon

on the choice of colour for the Model T Ford:
Any colour—so long as it's black.
  Henry Ford

It's just my colour: it's *beige*!
  Elsie Mendl, *a fashionable interior decorator's first view of the Parthenon*

If I could find anything blacker than black, I'd use it.
  J. M. W. Turner

Pink is the navy blue of India.
  Diana Vreeland

I think it pisses God off if you walk by the colour purple in a field somewhere and don't notice it.
Alice Walker

Computers

> ❝ To err is human but to really foul things up requires a computer. ❞
>
> **ANONYMOUS**

A modern computer hovers between the obsolescent and the nonexistent.
Sydney Brenner

On the Internet, nobody knows you're a dog.
Peter Steiner, *cartoon showing a large dog at a desk, paw on keyboard, enlightening a smaller friend*

We've all heard that a million monkeys banging on a million typewriters will eventually reproduce the entire works of Shakespeare. Now, thanks to the Internet, we know this is not true.
Robert Wilensky

I should prefer to have a politician who regularly went to a massage parlour than one who promised a laptop computer for every teacher.

A. N. Wilson

Conversation

66 Too much agreement kills a chat. 99

ELDRIDGE CLEAVER

Is it possible to cultivate the art of conversation when living in the country all the year round?

E. M. Delafield

How time flies when you's doin' all the talking.

Harvey Fierstein

If you are ever at a loss to support a flagging conversation, introduce the subject of eating.

Leigh Hunt

The opposite of talking isn't listening. The opposite of talking is waiting.

Fran Lebowitz

on George Bernard Shaw's wife as a good listener:
God knows she had plenty of practice.
   J. B. Priestley

Faith, that's as well said, as if I had said it myself.
   Jonathan Swift

I re-iterate. You remember, I iterated before.
   Dick Vosburgh

If one plays good music, people don't listen and if one
plays bad music people don't talk.
   Oscar Wilde

Cookery

66 Be content to remember that those who
can make omelettes properly can do
nothing else. 99

HILAIRE BELLOC

I really am too lazy to make radish roses, even if I like
them.
   Lee Bailey

Anyone who tells a lie has not a pure heart, and cannot make a good soup.

Ludwig van Beethoven

My mother tells me she's worn out pouring tinned sauce over the frozen chicken.

Maeve Binchy

That's not an act of love. It's an act of hate.

Raymond Blanc, *on English food*

The discovery of a new dish does more for the happiness of mankind than the discovery of a new star.

Anthelme Brillat-Savarin

A cucumber should be well sliced, and dressed with pepper and vinegar, and then thrown out, as good for nothing.

Samuel Johnson

It has nothing to do with frogs' legs. No amphibian is harmed in the making of this dish.

Nigella Lawson, *explaining toad-in-the-hole to Americans*

Sorry, I don't do offal.

Jamie Oliver, *invited to help improve the food in the Westminster kitchens*

The cook was a good cook, as cooks go; and as cooks go, she went.

Saki

You won't be surprised that diseases are innumerable— count the cooks.

Seneca

I want to focus on my salad.

Martha Stewart, *when questioned on the 'Early Show' about a congressional investigation into her sale of shares*

The most remarkable thing about my mother is that for 30 years she served nothing but leftovers. The original meal was never found.

Tracey Ullman

Cricket

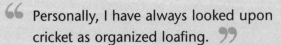

Personally, I have always looked upon cricket as organized loafing.

WILLIAM TEMPLE

contributing to W. G. Grace's testimonial:
It's not in support of cricket but as an earnest protest against golf.
Max Beerbohm

The last positive thing England did for cricket was invent it.
Ian Chappell

I couldn't bat for the length of time required to score 500. I'd get bored and fall over.
Denis Compton

Never read print, it spoils one's eye for the ball.
W. G. Grace, *habitual advice to his players*

Cricket—a game which the English, not being a spiritual people, have invented in order to give themselves some conception of eternity.

Lord Mancroft

Cricket is basically baseball on valium.

Robin Williams

Crime

> 66 Major Strasser has been shot. Round up the usual suspects. 99
>
> JULIUS J. EPSTEIN ET AL.

Office supplies are an important part of your total compensation package. If God didn't want people to steal office supplies he wouldn't have given us briefcases, purses, and pockets.

Scott Adams, *Dilbert's approach*

to a prison visitor who asked if he were sewing:
No, reaping.

Horatio Bottomley

What is robbing a bank compared with founding a bank?
   Bertolt Brecht

Thieves respect property. They merely wish the property to
become their property that they may more perfectly
respect it.
   G. K. Chesterton

It is quite a three-pipe problem, and I beg that you won't
speak to me for fifty minutes.
   Arthur Conan Doyle, *Sherlock Holmes to Dr Watson*

Something lingering, with boiling oil in it, I fancy.
   W. S. Gilbert

It was beautiful and simple as all truly great swindles are.
   O. Henry

When I heard the words criminal investigation my mindset
changed considerably.
   Oliver North

Diaries

> 66 I always say, keep a diary and some day it'll keep you. 99
>
> **MAE WEST**

A page of my Journal is like a cake of portable soup. A little may be diffused into a considerable portion.

James Boswell

What is more dull than a discreet diary? One might just as well have a discreet soul.

Chips Channon

To write a diary every day is like returning to one's own vomit.

Enoch Powell

I have decided to keep a full journal, in the hope that my life will perhaps seem more interesting when it is written down.

Sue Townsend, *Adrian Mole*

I never travel without my diary. One should always have
something sensational to read in the train.

Oscar Wilde, *Gwendolen's custom*

Diplomacy

> We exchanged many frank words in our
> respective languages.
>
> **PETER COOK**

American *diplomacy*. It's like watching somebody trying to
do joinery with a chainsaw.

James Hamilton-Paterson

There cannot be a crisis next week. My schedule is already
full.

Henry Kissinger

The French are masters of 'the dog ate my homework'
school of diplomatic relations.

P. J. O'Rourke

The chief distinction of a diplomat is that he can say no in such a way that it sounds like yes.

Lester Bowles Pearson

A diplomat these days is nothing but a head-waiter who's allowed to sit down occasionally.

Peter Ustinov

An ambassador is an honest man sent to lie abroad for the good of his country.

Henry Wotton

Drink

> 66 A woman drove me to drink and I never even had the courtesy to thank her. 99
>
> **W. C. FIELDS**

He summoned a cabin steward and ordered a glass of whisky, and nursed it as if it were very ill indeed.

Douglas Adams

I saw a notice which said 'Drink Canada Dry' and I've just started.
   Brendan Behan

Often Daddy sat up very late working on a case of Scotch.
   Robert Benchley

I have taken more out of alcohol than alcohol has taken out of me.
   Winston Churchill

'I rather like bad wine,' said Mr Mountchesney; 'one gets so bored with good wine.'
   Benjamin Disraeli

Some weasel took the cork out of my lunch.
   W. C. Fields

I always keep a supply of stimulant handy in case I see a snake—which I also keep handy.
   W. C. Fields

There is no such thing as a small whisky.
   Oliver St John Gogarty

Love makes the world go round? Not at all. Whisky makes it go round twice as fast.
   Compton Mackenzie

You're not drunk if you can lie on the floor without holding on.
   Dean Martin

One more drink and I'd have been under the host.
   Dorothy Parker

A good general rule is to state that the bouquet is better than the taste, and vice versa.
   Stephen Potter, *on wine-tasting*

I'm only a beer teetotaller, not a champagne teetotaller.
   George Bernard Shaw

Good God! I've never drunk a vintage that starts with the number two before.
   Nicholas Soames

It's a naïve domestic Burgundy without any breeding, but I think you'll be amused by its presumption.
   James Thurber

What have you been doing in my absinthe?
   Dick Vosburgh

I have a rare intolerance to herbs which means I can only drink fermented liquids, such as gin.
   Julie Walters

It was my Uncle George who discovered that alcohol was a food well in advance of medical thought.

P. G. Wodehouse

Drugs

> 66 Reality is a crutch for people who can't cope with drugs. 99
>
> LILY TOMLIN

LSD? Nothing much happened, but I did get the distinct impression that some birds were trying to communicate with me.

W. H. Auden

Cocaine habit-forming? Of course not. I ought to know. I've been using it for years.

Tallulah Bankhead

I'll die young, but it's like kissing God.

Lenny Bruce

I experimented with marijuana a time or two. And I didn't like it, and I didn't inhale.

Bill Clinton

Drugs have taught an entire generation of English kids the metric system.

P. J. O'Rourke

Sure thing, man. I used to be a laboratory myself once.

Keith Richards, *on being asked to autograph a fan's school chemistry book*

Economics

66 Greed—for lack of a better word—is good. Greed is right. Greed works. 99

STANLEY WEISER AND OLIVER STONE

No real English gentleman, in his secret soul, was ever sorry for the death of a political economist.

Walter Bagehot

It's the economy, stupid.
> **James Carville,** *on a sign put up at the 1992 Clinton presidential campaign headquarters*

I never could make out what those damned dots meant.
> **Lord Randolph Churchill,** *as Chancellor, on decimal points*

Trickle-down theory—the less than elegant metaphor that if one feeds the horse enough oats, some will pass through to the road for the sparrows.
> **J. K. Galbraith**

Balancing the budget is like going to heaven. Everybody wants to do it, but nobody wants to do what you have to do to get there.
> **Phil Gramm**

If economists could manage to get themselves thought of as humble, competent people, on a level with dentists, that would be splendid!
> **John Maynard Keynes**

Expenditure rises to meet income.
> **C. Northcote Parkinson**

I trust Bush with my daughter, but I trust Clinton with my job.
> **Craig Paterson**

Education

> 66 I read Shakespeare and the Bible and I can shoot dice. That's what I call a liberal education. 99
>
> **TALLULAH BANKHEAD**

I went to public school, of course. But looking back on it, I think it may have been Borstal.

Alan Bennett

No academic person is ever voted into the chair until he has reached an age at which he has forgotten the meaning of the word 'irrelevant'.

Francis M. Cornford

That state of resentful coma that...dons dignify by the name of research.

Harold Laski

If you are truly serious about preparing your child for the future, don't teach him to subtract—teach him to deduct.

Fran Lebowitz

At school I never minded the lessons. I just resented having to work terribly hard at playing.

John Mortimer

The schoolteacher is certainly underpaid as a childminder, but ludicrously overpaid as an educator.

John Osborne

For every person who wants to teach there are approximately thirty who don't want to learn—much.

W. C. Sellar and R. J. Yeatman

He who can, does. He who cannot, teaches.

George Bernard Shaw

I am putting old heads on your young shoulders...all my pupils are the crème de la crème.

Muriel Spark

'We class schools, you see, into four grades: Leading School, First-rate School, Good School, and School. Frankly,' said Mr Levy, 'School is pretty bad.'

Evelyn Waugh

Fame

> ❝ You can't shame or humiliate modern celebrities. What used to be called shame and humiliation is now called publicity. ❞
>
> **P. J. O'ROURKE**

A celebrity is a person who works hard all his life to become well known, and then wears dark glasses to avoid being recognized.
Fred Allen

I go in and out of fashion like a double-breasted suit.
Alan Ayckbourn

Oh, the self-importance of fading stars. Never mind, they will be black holes one day.
Jeffrey Bernard

Fancy being remembered around the world for the invention of a mouse!
Walt Disney

The transition from Who's Who to Who's He.
Eddie George, *on retirement*

The best fame is a writer's fame: it's enough to get a table at a good restaurant, but not enough that you get interrupted when you eat.
Fran Lebowitz

I'm world famous, Dr Parks said, all over Canada.
Mordecai Richler

Well, not exactly a big star...But I once had a sandwich named after me at the Stage Delicatessen.
Neil Simon

One day you're a signature, next day you're an autograph.
Billy Wilder

The Family

> If a man's character is to be abused, say what you will, there's nobody like a relation to do the business.
>
> **WILLIAM MAKEPEACE THACKERAY**

My mother-in-law broke up my marriage. My wife came home from work one day and found us in bed together.
 Lenny Bruce

You know what they say, if at first you don't succeed, you're not the eldest son.
 Stephen Fry

A home keeps you from living with your parents.
 P. J. O'Rourke

It is a wise father that knows his own child.
 William Shakespeare

We have become a grandmother.
 Margaret Thatcher

I'm Charley's aunt from Brazil—where the nuts come from.
Brandon Thomas

All happy families resemble one another, but each unhappy family is unhappy in its own way.
Leo Tolstoy

I have four sons and three stepsons. I have learnt what it is like to step on Lego with bare feet.
Fay Weldon

To lose one parent, Mr Worthing, may be regarded as a misfortune; to lose both looks like carelessness.
Oscar Wilde

It is no use telling me that there are bad aunts and good aunts. At the core, they are all alike. Sooner or later, out pops the cloven hoof.
P. G. Wodehouse

Occasions when Aunt is calling to Aunt like mastodons bellowing across primeval swamps.
P. G. Wodehouse

Fashion

> ❝ I never cared for fashion much. Amusing little seams and witty little pleats. It was the girls I liked. ❞
>
> **DAVID BAILEY**

It is totally impossible to be well dressed in cheap shoes.
   Hardy Amies

When he buys his ties he has to ask if gin will make them run.
   F. Scott Fitzgerald

I want people to look at the woman wearing my clothes and think, 'She's having an affair'.
   Katherine Hamnett

You should never have your best trousers on when you go out to fight for freedom and truth.
   Henrik Ibsen

when a waiter at Buckingham Palace spilled soup on her dress:
Never darken my Dior again!
   Beatrice Lillie

A woman's dress should be like a barbed wire fence: serving
its purpose without obstructing the view.
   Sophia Loren

The American tourist abroad...wears clothes suitable for a
trip to a disaster area, or for a visit to a museum or zoo.
   Alison Lurie

on being asked what she wore in bed:
Chanel No. 5.
   Marilyn Monroe

Fur is a subject that makes sensitive toes curl in their
leather shoes.
   Jeremy Paxman

I wish I had invented blue jeans.
   Yves Saint Laurent, *on his only regret*

His socks compelled one's attention without losing one's
respect.
   Saki

Her frocks are built in Paris, but she wears them with a strong English accent.
Saki

If Botticelli were alive today he'd be working for *Vogue*.
Peter Ustinov

I like to dress egos. If you haven't got an ego today, you can forget it.
Gianni Versace

Food

66 Cauliflower is nothing but cabbage with a college education. 99

MARK TWAIN

I've eaten shepherd's pie at The Ivy and the Savoy, but I've never seen anything like Belmarsh's version.
Jeffrey Archer

A gourmet can tell from the flavour whether a woodcock's leg is the one on which the bird is accustomed to roost.
Lucius Beebe

Some of the waiters discuss the menu with you as if they were sharing wisdom picked up in the Himalayas.
Seymour Britchky

Take away that pudding—it has no theme.
Winston Churchill

[Cheese is] milk's leap toward immortality.
Clifton Fadiman

Roast Beef, Medium, is not only a food. It is a philosophy.
Edna Ferber

Of soup and love, the first is the best.
Thomas Fuller

I ate his liver with some fava beans and a nice chianti.
Thomas Harris and Ted Tally

The piece of cod passeth all understanding.
Edwin Lutyens

to a friend who had said that he hated English food:
All you have to do is eat breakfast three times a day.
W. Somerset Maugham

explaining her dislike of soup:
I do not believe in building a meal on a lake.
  Elsie Mendl

There was greasy toad in an equally greasy hole, and a
bacon and egg pie so dry and powdery that it was like
eating a crumbling 17th-century wattle and daub cottage.
  David Nobbs, *description of the wartime food at his prep school*

Never serve oysters in a month that has no paycheck in it.
  P. J. O'Rourke

It is said that the effect of eating too much lettuce is
'soporific'.
  Beatrix Potter

We always eat Oxford marmalade at Camblidge. Better
scholars, better plofessors at Camblidge, but better
marmalade at Oxford.
  Arthur Ransome

Like a purée of white kid gloves.
  Philip Sassoon, *of a dish of lobster Newburg*

'Turbot, Sir,' said the waiter, placing before me two
fishbones, two eyeballs, and a bit of black mackintosh.
  Thomas Earle Welby

Beulah, peel me a grape.
  Mae West

MOTHER: It's broccoli, dear.
CHILD: I say it's spinach, and I say the hell with it.
  E. B. White

When I ask for a watercress sandwich, I do not mean a loaf
with a field in the middle of it.
  Oscar Wilde

What with excellent browsing and sluicing and cheery
conversation and what-not, the afternoon passed quite
happily.
  P. G. Wodehouse

One doughnut doesn't do a thing. You've got to eat 20 a
day for five weeks before you get results.
  Renee Zellweger, *preparing to play Bridget Jones*

Foolishness

> ❝ As any fule kno. ❞
> **GEOFFREY WILLANS AND RONALD SEARLE**

Mr Kremlin himself was distinguished for ignorance, for he had only one idea,—and that was wrong.

Benjamin Disraeli

A man may be a fool and not know it, but not if he is married.

H. L. Mencken

Seriousness is stupidity sent to college.

P. J. O'Rourke

You stupid boy!

Jimmy Perry and David Croft, *Captain Mainwaring to Private Pike, in* Dad's Army

Hain't we got all the fools in town on our side? and ain't that a big enough majority in any town?

Mark Twain

Better to keep your mouth shut and appear stupid than to open it and remove all doubt.

Mark Twain

Ignorance is like a delicate exotic fruit; touch it and the bloom is gone.

Oscar Wilde

Football

66 The natural state of the football fan is bitter disappointment, no matter what the score. 99

NICK HORNBY

I hate manly men. Four men in a car talking about football is my idea of hell.

David Bailey

Football's football; if that weren't the case, it wouldn't be the game it is.

Garth Crooks

Never mind football! Try parliamentary democracry!
Michael Frayn

I got into moisturiser when I played football. If you're out in all weathers you have to take care of your face.
Vinnie Jones

Some people think football is a matter of life and death...I can assure them it is much more serious than that.
Bill Shankly

We're having a philosophical discussion about the yob ethics of professional footballers.
Tom Stoppard

Friendship

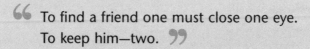

66 To find a friend one must close one eye.
To keep him—two. 99

NORMAN DOUGLAS

I may be wrong, but I have never found deserting friends conciliates enemies.
Margot Asquith

Champagne for my real friends, and real pain for my sham friends.

Francis Bacon, *a favourite toast*

If I were God and I were trying to create a nation that would get up the nostril of the Englishman I would create the French.

Julian Barnes

[Friends are] God's apology for relations.

Hugh Kingsmill

Money couldn't buy friends but you got a better class of enemy.

Spike Milligan

If it is abuse,—why one is always sure to hear of it from one damned goodnatured friend or another!

Richard Brinsley Sheridan

I am a hoarder of two things: documents and trusted friends.

Muriel Spark

I regard you with an indifference closely bordering on aversion.

Robert Louis Stevenson

Hello, I'm Julian and this is my friend, Sandy.

Barry Took and Marty Feldman, *customary introduction by the resting actors of* Round the Horne

It takes your enemy and your friend, working together, to hurt you to the heart: the one to slander you and the other to get the news to you.

Mark Twain

He [Bernard Shaw] hasn't an enemy in the world, and none of his friends like him.

Oscar Wilde

 # The Future

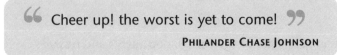 66 Cheer up! the worst is yet to come! 99

PHILANDER CHASE JOHNSON

That period of time in which our affairs prosper, our friends are true, and our happiness is assured.

Ambrose Bierce

Posterity is as likely to be wrong as anybody else.

Heywood Broun

I never think of the future. It comes soon enough.
   Albert Einstein

You can only predict things after they have happened.
   Eugène Ionesco

Soon we'll be sliding down the razor-blade of life.
   Tom Lehrer

Gambling

66 I long ago come to the conclusion that all life is 6 to 5 against. 99
   DAMON RUNYON

I have a notion that gamblers are as happy as most people—being always excited.
   Lord Byron

Rowe's Rule: the odds are five to six that the light at the end of the tunnel is the headlight of an oncoming train.
   Paul Dickson

Never give a sucker an even break.
W. C. Fields

GAMBLER: Say, is this a game of chance?
CUTHBERT J. TWILLIE: Not the way I play it.
W. C. Fields

The Generation Gap

> 66 It is the one war in which everyone
> changes sides. 99
>
> **CYRIL CONNOLLY**

They're both on drugs, they both detest you, and neither of
them have got a job.
Jasper Carrott, *comparing teenagers and grandparents*

When I was young, the old regarded me as an outrageous
young fellow, and now that I'm old the young regard me as
an outrageous old fellow.
Fred Hoyle

What is a teenager in San Francisco to rebel against, for pity's sake? Their parents are all so busy trying to be non-judgemental, it's no wonder they take to dyeing their hair green.

Molly Ivins

Grown-ups never understand anything for themselves, and it is tiresome for children to be always and forever explaining things to them.

Antoine de Saint-Exupéry

The young have aspirations that never come to pass, the old have reminiscences of what never happened.

Saki

The denunciation of the young is a necessary part of the hygiene of older people, and greatly assists the circulation of their blood.

Logan Pearsall Smith

There is more felicity on the far side of baldness than young men can possibly imagine.

Logan Pearsall Smith

When I was a boy of 14, my father was so ignorant I could hardly stand to have the old man around. But when I got to be 21, I was astonished at how much the old man had learned in seven years.

Mark Twain

God

> **❝** God is not dead but alive and working on a much less ambitious project. **❞**
>
> **ANONYMOUS**

If only God would give me some clear sign! Like making a large deposit in my name at a Swiss bank.
   Woody Allen

I expect to see God in a five-button suit.
   Hardy Amies

An apology for the Devil: It must be remembered that we have only heard one side of the case. God has written all the books.
   Samuel Butler

I'm sorry, we don't do God.
   Alastair Campbell, *when Tony Blair was asked about his Christian faith in an interview*

He's not the Messiah! He's a very naughty boy!
   John Cleese et al., *Brian's mother to his would-be followers*

Our only hope rests on the off-chance that God does exist.
   Alice Thomas Ellis

God was left out of the Constitution but was furnished a front seat on the coins of the country.
   Mark Twain

Golf

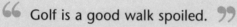

66 Golf is a good walk spoiled. 99

MARK TWAIN

If you watch a game, it's fun. If you play it, it's recreation. If you work at it, it's golf.
   Bob Hope

I'm playing like Tarzan and scoring like Jane.
   Chi Chi Rodrigues

The uglier a man's legs are, the better he plays golf—it's almost a law.
   H. G. Wells

The least thing upset him on the links. He missed short putts because of the uproar of the butterflies in the adjoining meadows.

P. G. Wodehouse

Gossip

> If you haven't got anything good to say about anyone come and sit by me.
>
> **ALICE ROOSEVELT LONGWORTH**

It's the gossip columnist's business to write about what is none of his business.

Louis Kronenberger

I hate to spread rumours, but what else can one do with them?

Amanda Lear

Gossip is what you say about the objects of flattery when they aren't present.

P. J. O'Rourke

You have dished me up, like a savoury omelette, to gratify the appetite of the reading rabble for gossip.
  Thomas Love Peacock

I hope there's a tinge of disgrace about me. Hopefully, there's one good scandal left in me yet.
  Diana Rigg

Here is the whole set! a character dead at every word.
  Richard Brinsley Sheridan

There is only one thing in the world worse than being talked about, and that is not being talked about.
  Oscar Wilde

Gossip is hearing something you like about someone you don't.
  Earl Wilson

Government

> A government which robs Peter to pay Paul can always depend on the support of Paul.
>
> **GEORGE BERNARD SHAW**

Like most Chief Whips he [Michael Jopling] knew who the shits were.

Alan Clark

Distrust of authority should be the first civic duty.

Norman Douglas

People must not do things for fun. We are not here for fun. There is no reference to fun in any Act of Parliament.

A. P. Herbert

Office hours are from 12 to 1 with an hour off for lunch.

George S. Kaufman, *of the US Senate*

How is the world ruled and how do wars start? Diplomats tell lies to journalists and then believe what they read.

Karl Kraus

Office tends to confer a dreadful plausibility on even the most negligible of those who hold it.
   Mark Lawson

One of these days the people of Louisiana are going to get good government—and they aren't going to like it.
   Huey Long

Whatever it is that the government does, sensible Americans would prefer that the government does it to somebody else. This is the idea behind foreign policy.
   P. J. O'Rourke

We all know that Prime Ministers are wedded to the truth, but like other married couples they sometimes live apart.
   Saki

I don't mind how much my Ministers talk, so long as they do what I say.
   Margaret Thatcher

of his first Cabinet meeting as Prime Minister:
An extraordinary affair. I gave them their orders and they wanted to stay and discuss them.
   Duke of Wellington

Handwriting

> The dawn of legibility in his handwriting has revealed his utter inability to spell.
>
> **IAN HAY**

That exquisite handwriting like a fly which has been trained at the Russian ballet.

James Agate, *of George Bernard Shaw's handwriting*

No individual word was decipherable, but, with a bold reader, groups could be made to conform to a scheme based on probabilities.

Edith Œ. Somerville and Martin Ross

I know that handwriting...I remember it perfectly. The ten commandments in every stroke of the pen, and the moral law all over the page.

Oscar Wilde

Happiness

> **All the things I really like to do are either illegal, immoral, or fattening.**
>
> **ALEXANDER WOOLLCOTT**

No pleasure is worth giving up for the sake of two more years in a geriatric home in Weston-super-Mare.

Kingsley Amis

Mr Bennet dissuading his daughter Mary from continuing to sing:
You have delighted us long enough.

Jane Austen

I can tolerate without discomfort being waited on hand and foot.

Osbert Lancaster

I can imagine no more comfortable frame of mind for the conduct of life than a humorous resignation.

W. Somerset Maugham

He's simply got the instinct for being unhappy highly developed.

Saki

There are two tragedies in life. One is not to get your heart's desire. The other is to get it.

George Bernard Shaw

Life would be very pleasant if it were not for its enjoyments.

R. S. Surtees

Health

66 I feel as young as I ever did, apart from the occasional heart attack. 99

ROBERT BENCHLEY

Keep paying the electricity bill.

Anonymous, *doctor's advice after Roger Moore was fitted with a pacemaker*

The two best exercises in the world are making love and dancing but a simple one is to stand on tiptoe.

Barbara Cartland

Exercise is the yuppie version of bulimia.

Barbara Ehrenreich

You die of a heart attack but so what? You die thin.

Bob Geldof, *on the Atkins diet*

It's no longer a question of staying healthy. It's a question of finding a sickness you like.

Jackie Mason

The only exercise I take is walking behind the coffins of friends who took exercise.

Peter O'Toole

I am on two diets at the moment. Because you don't get enough to eat with one.

Peter Sessions

I try to keep fit. I've got these parallel bars at home. I run at them and try to buy a drink from both of them.

Arthur Smith

 **History**

  History is more or less bunk.

HENRY FORD

History repeats itself; historians repeat one other.
Rupert Brooke

People who make history know nothing about history. You can see that in the sort of history they make.
G. K. Chesterton

History teaches us that men and nations behave wisely once they have exhausted all other alternatives.
Abba Eban

I grew up in Europe, where the history comes from.
Eddie Izzard

History is not what you thought. *It is what you can remember.*
W. C. Sellar and R. J. Yeatman

AMERICA was thus clearly top nation, and History came to a .
W. C. Sellar and R. J. Yeatman

History gets thicker as it approaches recent times.
A. J. P. Taylor

Human history becomes more and more a race between education and catastrophe.
H. G. Wells

The one duty we owe to history is to rewrite it.
Oscar Wilde

History started badly and hav been geting steadily worse.
Geoffrey Willans and Ronald Searle

The Home

> All I need is room enough to lay a hat and a few friends.
>
> **DOROTHY PARKER**

Conran's Law of Housework—it expands to fill the time available plus half an hour.
  Shirley Conran

There was no need to do any housework at all. After the first four years the dirt doesn't get any worse.
  Quentin Crisp

There's no greater bliss in life than when the plumber eventually comes to unblock your drains. No writer can give that sort of pleasure.
  Victoria Glendinning

A dog in the home is a piece of moving furniture.
  Philippe de Rothschild

Home life as we understand it is no more natural to us than a cage is natural to a cockatoo.

George Bernard Shaw

It looks different when you're sober. I thought I had twice as much furniture.

Neil Simon

Hatred of domestic work is a natural and admirable result of civilization.

Rebecca West

The Human Race

We used to build civilizations. Now we build shopping malls.

BILL BRYSON

Well, of course, people are only human...But it really does not seem much for them to be.

Ivy Compton-Burnett

I got disappointed in human nature as well and gave it up because I found it too much like my own.

J. P. Donleavy

Men have an extraordinarily erroneous opinion of their position in nature; and the error is ineradicable.

W. Somerset Maugham

Man is one of the toughest of animated creatures. Only the anthrax bacillus can stand so unfavourable an environment for so long a time.

H. L. Mencken

I'm dealing in rock'n'roll. I'm, like, I'm not a bona fide human being.

Phil Spector

The only man who wasn't spoilt by being lionized was Daniel.

Herbert Beerbohm Tree

Man is the Only Animal that Blushes. Or needs to.

Mark Twain

Humour

> **66** Without humour you cannot run a
> sweetie-shop, let alone a nation. **99**
>
> **JOHN BUCHAN**

The marvellous thing about a joke with a double meaning
is that it can only mean one thing.
   Ronnie Barker

Mark my words, when a society has to resort to the
lavatory for its humour, the writing is on the wall.
   Alan Bennett

The role of humour is to make people fall down and writhe
on the Axminster, and that is the top and bottom of it.
   Alan Coren

The trouble with Freud is that he never had to play the old
Glasgow Empire on a Saturday night after Rangers and
Celtic had both lost.
   Ken Dodd

A difference of taste in jokes is a great strain on the affections.
George Eliot

Comedy, like sodomy, is an unnatural act.
Marty Feldman

There's a weight of intellect behind my comedy.
Ricky Gervais and Stephen Merchant, *David Brent as humorist*

'Tis ever thus with simple folk—an accepted wit has but to say 'Pass the mustard', and they roar their ribs out!
W. S. Gilbert

What do you mean, funny? Funny-peculiar or funny ha-ha?
Ian Hay

I was born in Melbourne with a priceless gift. It was the ability—the priceless ability—to laugh at the misfortunes of others.
Barrie Humphries

You need real surprise. It's like poetry. A good joke turns life inside out.
Terry Jones

It's an odd job, making decent people laugh.
Molière

They laughed when I said I was going to be a
comedian...They're not laughing now.
   Bob Monkhouse

Laughter is pleasant, but the exertion is too much for me.
   Thomas Love Peacock

Everything is funny as long as it is happening to Somebody
Else.
   Will Rogers

There are three basic rules for great comedy. Unfortunately
no-one can remember what they are.
   Arthur Smith

For every ten jokes, thou hast got an hundred enemies.
   Laurence Sterne

It would be a sad reflection on any satirical programme if
no one ended up taking offence at some point.
   Meera Syal

Humour is emotional chaos remembered in tranquillity.
   James Thurber

Laughter would be bereaved if snobbery died.
   Peter Ustinov

Madeleine Bassett laughed the tinkling, silvery laugh that had got her so disliked by the better element.

P. G. Wodehouse

Ideas

> 66 The English approach to ideas is not to kill them, but to let them die of neglect. 99
>
> **JEREMY PAXMAN**

I ran into Isosceles. He has a great idea for a new triangle!

Woody Allen

I have a cunning plan.

Richard Curtis and Ben Elton, *Baldrick's habitual overoptimistic promise to Blackadder*

An original idea. That can't be too hard. The library must be full of them.

Stephen Fry

I had a monumental idea this morning, but I didn't like it.

Sam Goldwyn

It is better to entertain an idea than to take it home to live with you for the rest of your life.
   Randall Jarrell

When the inventor of the drawing-board messed up, what did he go back to?
   Bob Monkhouse

There are some ideas so wrong that only a very intelligent person could believe in them.
   George Orwell

Insults

> 66 I never forget a face, but in your case I'll be glad to make an exception. 99
>
> **GROUCHO MARX**

The *t* is silent, as in *Harlow*.
   Margot Asquith, *to Jean Harlow, who had been mispronouncing her first name*

NANCY ASTOR: If I were your wife I would put poison in your coffee!
WINSTON CHURCHILL: And if I were your husband I would drink it.
Nancy Astor

[Clement Attlee is] a modest man who has a good deal to be modest about.
Winston Churchill

on being criticized by Geoffrey Howe:
Like being savaged by a dead sheep.
Denis Healey

So dumb he can't fart and chew gum at the same time.
Lyndon Baines Johnson, *of Gerald Ford*

The trouble with Michael is that he had to buy all his furniture.
Michael Jopling, *of Michael Heseltine*

Causing offence is important and beneficial to humanity. People should be offended three times a week and twice on Sundays.
John Mortimer

on being told that Clare Boothe Luce was always kind to her inferiors:
And where does she find them?
Dorothy Parker

I am not offended by dumb blonde jokes because I know that I'm not dumb. I also know that I'm not a blonde.
Dolly Parton

I only say what the rest of you are thinking...It's the viewer's job to be shocked and pretend it's terrible.
Anne Robinson

JUDGE: You are extremely offensive, young man.
SMITH: As a matter of fact, we both are, and the only difference between us is that I am trying to be, and you can't help it.
F. E. Smith

" Intelligence

66 Genius is one per cent inspiration, ninety-nine per cent perspiration. 99
THOMAS ALVA EDISON

Men of genius are so few that they ought to atone for their fewness by being at any rate ubiquitous.
Max Beerbohm

I think, therefore I am is the statement of an intellectual who underrates toothaches.
  Milan Kundera

I don't think there's intelligent life on other planets. Why should other planets be any different from this one?
  Bob Monkhouse

A genius. An I.Q. of 170. Same as her weight.
  Neil Simon

What is a highbrow? He is a man who has found something more interesting than women.
  Edgar Wallace

I have nothing to declare except my genius.
  Oscar Wilde

'Well, I think you're a pig.'
'A pig, maybe, but a shrewd, levelheaded pig. I wouldn't touch the project with a bargepole.'
  P. G. Wodehouse

Journalism

> When seagulls follow a trawler, it is because they think sardines will be thrown into the sea.
>
> **ERIC CANTONA**

When a dog bites a man, that is not news, because it happens so often. But if a man bites a dog, that is news.

John B. Bogart

Journalism largely consists in saying 'Lord Jones Dead' to people who never knew that Lord Jones was alive.

G. K. Chesterton

The first law of journalism—to confirm existing prejudice rather than contradict it.

Alexander Cockburn

If you lose your temper at a newspaper columnist, he'll be rich, or famous, or both.

James Hagerty, *the view of President Eisenhower's press secretary*

Power without responsibility: the prerogative of the harlot throughout the ages.
    Rudyard Kipling

Speaking for myself, if there is a message I want to be off it.
    Jeremy Paxman

Comment is free but facts are on expenses.
    Tom Stoppard

A journalist is somebody who possesses himself of a fantasy and lures the truth towards it.
    Arnold Wesker

Rock journalism is people who can't write interviewing people who can't talk for people who can't read.
    Frank Zappa

Language

> When I split an infinitive, God damn it, I split it so it will stay split.
>
> **RAYMOND CHANDLER**

I don't want to have to refer to my French fry potatoes as freedom fries, and I don't want to have to freedom kiss my wife.

Woody Allen

You know the trouble with the French, they don't even have a word for entrepreneur.

George W. Bush, *probably apocryphal*

This is the sort of English up with which I will not put.

Winston Churchill

Save the gerund and screw the whale.

Tom Stoppard

I was born to be a punctuation vigilante.

Lynne Truss

on the first-person plural pronoun:
Only presidents, editors, and people with tapeworms have the right to use the editorial 'we'.
Mark Twain

Good intentions are invariably ungrammatical.
Oscar Wilde

The Law

> 66 'If the law supposes that,' said Mr Bumble...'the law is a ass—a idiot.' 99
> **CHARLES DICKENS**

This contract is so one-sided that I am surprised to find it written on both sides of the paper.
Lord Evershed

Who is your career counsellor? Icarus?
John Goldsmith, *to a lawyer noted for firing his clients*

If you want to get ahead in this world get a lawyer—not a book.
Fran Lebowitz

However harmless a thing is, if the law forbids it most people will think it wrong.

W. Somerset Maugham

I don't know as I want a lawyer to tell me what I cannot do. I hire him to tell me how to do what I want to do.

J. P. Morgan

No brilliance is needed in the law. Nothing but common sense, and relatively clean finger nails.

John Mortimer

I have always noticed that any time a man can't come and settle with you without bringing his lawyer, why, look out for him.

Will Rogers

Some circumstantial evidence is very strong, as when you find a trout in the milk.

Henry David Thoreau

What chance has the ignorant, uncultivated liar against the educated expert? What chance have I...against a lawyer?

Mark Twain

Letters

> ❝ I am not a cautious letter-writer and generally say what comes uppermost at the moment. ❞
>
> **LORD BYRON**

It is wonderful how much news there is when people write every other day; if they wait for a month, there is nothing that seems worth telling.

O. Douglas

Like women's letters; all the pith is in the postscript.

William Hazlitt

I have made this [letter] longer than usual, only because I have not had the time to make it shorter.

Blaise Pascal

Laura's repeated assurances to me that she had both replied to your letter and that she was about to do so are, I think, characteristic of a mind at bay.

S. J. Perelman

A woman seldom writes her mind but in her postscript.
  Richard Steele

I don't wish to sign my name, though I am afraid
everybody will know who the writer is: one's style is one's
signature always.
  Oscar Wilde

Libraries

66 I've been drunk for about a week now,
and I thought it might sober me up to sit
in a library. 99

  F. SCOTT FITZGERALD

If you file your waste-paper basket for 50 years, you have a
public library.
  Tony Benn

There is nowhere in the world where sleep is so deep as in
the libraries of the House of Commons.
  Chips Channon

Mr Cobb took me into his library and showed me his books, of which he had a complete set.
 Ring Lardner

'Our library,' said the president, 'two hundred thousand volumes!' 'Aye,' said the minister, 'a powerful heap of rubbish, I'll be bound!'
 Stephen Leacock

The Librarian...liked people who loved and respected books, and the best way to do that, in the Librarian's opinion, was to leave them on the shelves where Nature intended them to be.
 Terry Pratchett

Lies

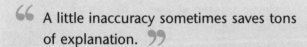

A little inaccuracy sometimes saves tons of explanation.

SAKI

It reminds me of the small boy who jumbled his biblical quotations and said: 'A lie is an abomination unto the Lord, and a very present help in trouble.'

Anonymous

She [Lady Desborough] tells enough white lies to ice a wedding cake.

Margot Asquith

That branch of the art of lying which consists in very nearly deceiving your friends without quite deceiving your enemies.

Francis M. Cornford, *of propaganda*

There are three kinds of lies: lies, damned lies and statistics.

Benjamin Disraeli

What you take for lying in an Irishman is only his attempt to put an herbaceous border on stark reality.
Oliver St John Gogarty

on being told that Lord Astor claimed that her allegations, concerning himself and his house parties at Cliveden, were untrue:
He would, wouldn't he?
Mandy Rice-Davies

I don't think the son of a bitch knows the difference between telling the truth and lying.
Harry S. Truman, *of Richard Nixon*

In exceptional circumstances it is necessary to say something that is untrue in the House of Commons.
William Waldegrave

Untruthful! My nephew Algernon? Impossible! He is an Oxonian.
Oscar Wilde

Life

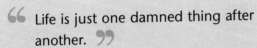

> Life is just one damned thing after another.
>
> ELBERT HUBBARD

Alun's life was coming to consist more and more exclusively of being told at dictation speed what he knew.

Kingsley Amis

Life is a sexually transmitted disease.

Anonymous

Never try to keep up with the Joneses. Drag them down to your level. It's cheaper that way.

Quentin Crisp

If A is a success in life, then A equals x plus y plus z. Work is x; y is play; and z is keeping your mouth shut.

Albert Einstein

Life is something to do when you can't get to sleep.

Fran Lebowitz

Life, if you're fat, is a minefield—you have to pick your way, otherwise you blow up.
   Miriam Margolyes

Laugh it off, laugh it off; it's all part of life's rich pageant.
   Arthur Marshall

I *love* living. I have some problems with my *life*, but living is the best thing they've come up with so far.
   Neil Simon

People say that life is the thing, but I prefer reading.
   Logan Pearsall Smith

Life is a gamble at terrible odds—if it was a bet, you wouldn't take it.
   Tom Stoppard

Oh, isn't life a terrible thing, thank God?
   Dylan Thomas

Literature

Literature's always a good card to play for Honours. It makes people think that Cabinet ministers are educated.

ARNOLD BENNETT

We were put to Dickens as children but it never quite took. That unremitting humanity soon had me cheesed off.

Alan Bennett

Dr Weiss, at forty, knew that her life had been ruined by literature.

Anita Brookner

If my books had been any worse, I should not have been invited to Hollywood, and if they had been any better, I should not have come.

Raymond Chandler

When I want to read a novel, I write one.

Benjamin Disraeli

He knew everything about literature except how to enjoy it.
Joseph Heller

Just Mills & Boon with Wonderbras.
Kathy Lette, *on Chicklit*

From the moment I picked up your book until I laid it down, I was convulsed with laughter. Some day I intend reading it.
Groucho Marx

You're familiar with the tragedies of antiquity, are you? The great homicidal classics?
Tom Stoppard

Do they keep throwing the book at Jeffrey Archer as an act of revenge for his lousy novels?
Keith Waterhouse

Love

 Even logical positivists are capable of love. 99

A. J. AYER

Women who love the same man have a kind of bitter freemasonry.

Max Beerbohm

Make love to every woman you meet. If you get five percent on your outlays it's a good investment.

Arnold Bennett

They made love as though they were an endangered species.

Peter de Vries

The magic of first love is our ignorance that it can ever end.

Benjamin Disraeli

I'm afraid I was very much the traditionalist. I went down on one knee and dictated a proposal which my secretary faxed over straight away.

Stephen Fry and Hugh Laurie

Love's like the measles—all the worse when it comes late in life.

Douglas Jerrold

Love's a disease. But curable.

Rose Macaulay

Love is the delusion that one woman differs from another.

H. L. Mencken

Kissing don't last: cookery do!

George Meredith

There are various ways of mending a broken heart, but perhaps going to a learned conference is one of the more unusual.

Barbara Pym

I was adored once too.

William Shakespeare

If love is the answer, could you rephrase the question?

Lily Tomlin

Love conquers all things—except poverty and toothache.
Mae West

To love oneself is the beginning of a lifelong romance.
Oscar Wilde

Marriage

> 66 Marriage is a wonderful invention; but,
> then again, so is a bicycle repair kit. 99
> **BILLY CONNOLLY**

If it were not for the presents, an elopement would be preferable.
George Ade

It was partially my fault that we got divorced...I tended to place my wife under a pedestal.
Woody Allen

[Marriage is] the only war where one sleeps with the enemy.
Anonymous

Bigamy is having one husband too many. Monogamy is the same.
Anonymous

It is a truth universally acknowledged, that a single man in possession of a good fortune, must be in want of a wife.
Jane Austen

A man cannot marry before he has studied anatomy and has dissected at the least one woman.
Honoré de Balzac

I'm not going to make the same mistake once.
Warren Beatty, *on choosing not to marry*

Being a husband is a whole-time job. That is why so many husbands fail. They cannot give their entire attention to it.
Arnold Bennett

Never marry a man who hates his mother, because he'll end up hating you.
Jill Bennett

Love matches are formed by people who pay for a month of honey with a life of vinegar.
Countess of Blessington

Even quarrels with one's husband are preferable to the ennui of a solitary existence.
   Elizabeth Patterson Bonaparte

I am about to be married—and am of course in all the misery of a man in pursuit of happiness.
   Lord Byron

The deep, deep peace of the double-bed after the hurly-burly of the chaise-longue.
   Mrs Patrick Campbell

The most happy marriage I can picture or imagine to myself would be the union of a deaf man to a blind woman.
   Samuel Taylor Coleridge

Marriage is a feast where the grace is sometimes better than the dinner.
   Charles Caleb Colton

There is no more sombre enemy of good art than the pram in the hall.
   Cyril Connolly

One of those looks which only a quarter-century of wedlock can adequately marinate.
   Alan Coren

I have always thought that every woman should marry, and no man.

Benjamin Disraeli

Being an old maid is like death by drowning, a really delightful sensation after you cease to struggle.

Edna Ferber

Maybe the Smug Marrieds only mix with other Smug Marrieds and don't know how to relate to individuals any more.

Helen Fielding, *Bridget Jones's view*

He taught me housekeeping; when I divorce I keep the house.

Zsa Zsa Gabor

when asked how many husbands she had had:
You mean apart from my own?

Zsa Zsa Gabor

The comfortable estate of widowhood, is the only hope that keeps up a wife's spirits.

John Gay

Do you think your mother and I should have lived comfortably so long together, if ever we had been married?

John Gay

I...chose my wife, as she did her wedding gown, not for a fine glossy surface, but such qualities as would wear well.

Oliver Goldsmith

My mother said it was simple to keep a man, you must be a maid in the living room, a cook in the kitchen and a whore in the bedroom. I said I'd hire the other two and take care of the bedroom bit.

Jerry Hall

The critical period in matrimony is breakfast-time.

A. P. Herbert

A TV host asked my wife, 'Have you ever considered divorce?' She replied: 'Divorce never, murder often.'

Charlton Heston

One doesn't have to get anywhere in a marriage. It's not a public conveyance.

Iris Murdoch

Marriage may often be a stormy lake, but celibacy is almost always a muddy horsepond.

Thomas Love Peacock

Strange to say what delight we married people have to see these poor fools decoyed into our condition.

Samuel Pepys

Advice to persons about to marry.—'Don't.'
  Punch

A husband is what is left of a lover, after the nerve has been extracted.
  Helen Rowland

Marriage is popular because it combines the maximum of temptation with the maximum of opportunity.
  George Bernard Shaw

'Tis safest in matrimony to begin with a little aversion.
  Richard Brinsley Sheridan

Even if we take matrimony at its lowest, even if we regard it as no more than a sort of friendship recognised by the police.
  Robert Louis Stevenson

Don't get mad, get everything.
  Ivana Trump, *advice to wronged wives*

Marriage isn't a word...it's a *sentence*!
  King Vidor

Marriage is a great institution, but I'm not ready for an institution yet.
  Mae West

GERRY: We can't get married at all...I'm a man.

OSGOOD: Well, nobody's perfect.

Billy Wilder and I. A. L. Diamond

Marriage is a bribe to make a housekeeper think she's a householder.

Thornton Wilder

Medicine

> 66 The desire to take medicine is perhaps the greatest feature which distinguishes man from animals. 99
>
> **WILLIAM OSLER**

I don't believe in vitamin pills. I swear by men, darling— and as many as possible.

Joan Collins

Any man who goes to a psychiatrist should have his head examined.

Sam Goldwyn

If you have a stomach ache, in France you get a suppository, in Germany a health spa, in the United States they cut your stomach open and in Britain they put you on a waiting list.

Phil Hammond and Michael Mosley

The kind of doctor I want is one who, when he's not examining me, is home studying medicine.

George S. Kaufman

In disease Medical Men guess: if they cannot ascertain a disease, they call it nervous.

John Keats

I only take Viagra when I'm with more than one woman.

Jack Nicholson

I fear that being a patient in any hospital in Ireland calls for two things—holy resignation and an iron constitution.

Flann O'Brien

There would never be any public agreement among doctors if they did not agree to agree on the main point of the doctor being always in the right.

George Bernard Shaw

There is at bottom only one genuinely scientific treatment for all diseases, and that is to stimulate the phagocytes.

George Bernard Shaw

Take anything that is either nasty, expensive or difficult to obtain, wrap it up in mystery and you have a cure.

Richard Totman

on being given aspirin from a small tin box by Jeeves:
Thank you, Jeeves. Don't slam the lid.

P. G. Wodehouse

The physician can bury his mistakes, but the architect can only advise his client to plant vines.

Frank Lloyd Wright

Men

66 My mother wanted me to be a nice boy. I didn't let her down. I don't smoke, drink or mess around with women. 99

JULIAN CLARY

We are lads. We have burgled houses and nicked car stereos, and we like girls and swear and go to the football and take the piss.

Noel Gallagher

Years ago, manhood was an opportunity for achievement, and now it is a problem to be overcome.
Garrison Keillor

The follies which a man regrets most, in his life, are those which he didn't commit when he had the opportunity.
Helen Rowland

God made him, and therefore let him pass for a man.
William Shakespeare

A hard man is good to find.
Mae West

There is something positively brutal about the good temper of most modern men.
Oscar Wilde

Men and Women

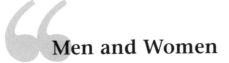

66 Women love scallywags, but some marry them and then try to make them wear a blazer. 99

DAVID BAILEY

Women were brought up to believe that men were the answer. They weren't. They weren't even one of the questions.

Julian Barnes

Women tend not to dress up in leather aprons and nail each other to coffee tables in their spare time.

Julie Burchill

The feminist movement seems to have beaten the manners out of men, but I didn't see them put up a lot of resistance.

Clarissa Dickson Wright

I will not...sulk about having no boyfriend, but develop inner poise and authority and sense of self as woman of substance, complete *without* boyfriend, as best way to obtain boyfriend.

Helen Fielding

A woman's mind is cleaner than a man's; she changes it more often.

Oliver Herford

Neanderthal. A glowering thug, the Terminator in shorts. And that's just my wife's opinion.

Martin Johnson

The female sex has no greater fan than I, and I have the bills to prove it.

Alan Jay Lerner

So then he said that he used to be a member of the choir himself, so who was he to cast the first rock at a girl like I.

Anita Loos

I suppose true sexual equality will come when a general called Anthea is found having an unwise lunch with a young, unreliable male model from Spain.

John Mortimer

A little incompatibility is the spice of life, particularly if he has income and she is pattable.

Ogden Nash

Twenty years ago when we had no respect for women they just used to say, 'You're chucked.' And now we do respect them we have to lie to them sensitively.

Simon Nye

Won't you come into the garden? I would like my roses to see you.

Richard Brinsley Sheridan, *to a young lady*

I don't want anyone to notice that I've been chucked, well, not even chucked, to be chucked you have to have been going out with someone, I've been...sort of sampled.

Arabella Weir

A man has one hundred dollars and you leave him with two dollars, that's subtraction.

Mae West

Is that a pistol in your pocket, or are you just glad to see me?

Mae West

When women go wrong, men go right after them.

Mae West

A man can be happy with any woman as long as he does not love her.

Oscar Wilde

All women become like their mothers. That is their tragedy. No man does. That's his.

Oscar Wilde

The others had their drugs and booze. I had my women. I thought that was safer: you can't overdose on women.

Bill Wyman

Middle Age

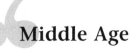

I recently turned 60. Practically a third of my life is over.

WOODY ALLEN

Years ago we discovered the exact point, the dead centre of middle age. It occurs when you are too young to take up golf and too old to rush up to the net.

Franklin P. Adams

Whenever the talk turns to age, I say I am 49 plus VAT.

Lionel Blair

After forty a woman has to choose between losing her figure or her face. My advice is to keep your face, and stay sitting down.

Barbara Cartland

As invariably happens after one passes 40, the paper sagged open to the obituary page.

S. J. Perelman

Maturity is a high price to pay for growing up.

Tom Stoppard

From birth to 18 a girl needs good parents. From 18 to 35, she needs good looks. From 35 to 55, good personality. From 55 on, she needs good cash.

Sophie Tucker

Thirty-five is a very attractive age. London society is full of women of the very highest birth who have, of their own free choice, remained thirty-five for years.

Oscar Wilde

Money

> I am in an age group where it is rude to discuss money, and now it is all anyone cares about.
>
> JACK NICHOLSON

Money is better than poverty, if only for financial reasons.
Woody Allen

Money, it turned out, was exactly like sex, you thought of nothing else if you didn't have it and thought of other things if you did.
James Baldwin

Money—the one thing that keeps us in touch with our children.
Gyles Brandreth

When you don't have any money, the problem is food. When you have money, it's sex. When you have both it's health.
J. P. Donleavy

Good news rarely comes in a brown envelope.

Henry D'Avigdor Goldsmid

on being told that money doesn't buy happiness:
But it upgrades despair so beautifully.

Richard Greenberg

Money is what you'd get on beautifully without if only other people weren't so crazy about it.

Margaret Case Harriman

A bank is a place that will lend you money if you can prove that you don't need it.

Bob Hope

There's only one thing to do with loose change of course. Tighten it.

Flann O'Brien

'My boy,' he says, 'always try to rub up against money, for if you rub up against money long enough, some of it may rub off on you.'

Damon Runyon

on being asked what Rosencrantz and Guildenstern are Dead *was about:*
It's about to make me very rich.

Tom Stoppard

Money won't buy happiness, but it will pay the salaries of a large research staff to study the problem.
Bill Vaughan

Morality

66 Moral indignation is jealousy with a halo. 99

H. G. WELLS

Morality's *not* practical. Morality's a gesture. A complicated gesture learned from books.
Robert Bolt

I probably have a different sense of morality to most people.
Alan Clark

I don't have a moral plan. I'm a Canadian.
David Cronenberg

To be absolutely honest, what I feel really bad about is that I don't feel worse. That's the ineffectual liberal's problem in a nutshell.

Michael Frayn

If people want a sense of purpose, they should get it from their archbishops. They should not hope to receive it from their politicians.

Harold Macmillan

Providing you have enough courage—or money—you can do without a reputation.

Margaret Mitchell, *said by Rhett Butler*

I think fidelity is a very good idea—now that I can't walk.

John Mortimer

People will do things from a sense of duty which they would never attempt as a pleasure.

Saki

Dost thou think, because thou art virtuous, there shall be no more cakes and ale?

William Shakespeare

When a stupid man is doing something he is ashamed of, he always declares that it is his duty.

George Bernard Shaw

On an occasion of this kind it becomes more than a moral duty to speak one's mind. It becomes a pleasure.

Oscar Wilde

 **Music**

> 66 Hell is full of musical amateurs: music is the brandy of the damned. 99
>
> **GEORGE BERNARD SHAW**

The music teacher came twice each week to bridge the awful gap between Dorothy and Chopin.

George Ade

I can't listen to too much Wagner, ya know? I start to get the urge to conquer Poland.

Woody Allen

printed notice in an American dancing saloon:
Please do not shoot the pianist. He is doing his best.

Anonymous

All music is folk music, I ain't never heard no horse sing a song.

Louis Armstrong

when asked what jazz is:
If you still have to ask...shame on you.

Louis Armstrong

There are two golden rules for an orchestra: start together and finish together. The public doesn't give a damn what goes on in between.

Thomas Beecham

Extraordinary how potent cheap music is.

Noël Coward

Playing 'Bop' is like scrabble with all the vowels missing.

Duke Ellington

I only know two tunes. One of them is 'Yankee Doodle' and the other isn't.

Ulysses S. Grant

I don't like my music, but what is my opinion against that of millions of others.

Frederick Loewe

If you're in jazz and more than ten people like you, you're labelled commercial.

Herbie Mann

I have been told that Wagner's music is better than it sounds.

Bill Nye

Wagner has lovely moments but awful quarters of an hour.

Gioacchino Rossini

I know two kinds of audiences only—one coughing, and one not coughing.

Artur Schnabel

I have a reasonable good ear in music: let us have the tongs and the bones.

William Shakespeare

Jazz will endure, just as long as people hear it through their feet instead of their brains.

John Philip Sousa

Newspapers

> 66 I'm with you on the free press. It's the newspapers I can't stand. 99
>
> **TOM STOPPARD**

I read the newspapers avidly. It is my one form of continuous fiction.

Aneurin Bevan

More than one newspaper has been ruined by the brilliant writer in the editor's chair.

Lord Camrose

Editor: a person employed by a newspaper, whose business it is to separate the wheat from the chaff, and to see that the chaff is printed.

Elbert Hubbard

People don't actually read newspapers. They get into them every morning, like a hot bath.

Marshall McLuhan

The art of newspaper paragraphing is to stroke a platitude until it purrs like an epigram.

Don Marquis

If a newspaper prints a sex crime, it is smut: but when the *New York Times* prints it it is a sociological study.

Adolph S. Ochs

Accuracy to a newspaper is what virtue is to a lady; but a newspaper can always print a retraction.

Adlai Stevenson

There are laws to protect the freedom of the press's speech, but none that are worth anything to protect the people from the press.

Mark Twain

The Beast stands for strong mutually antagonistic governments everywhere...Self-sufficiency at home, self-assertion abroad.

Evelyn Waugh

Newspapers, even, have degenerated. They may now be absolutely relied upon.

Oscar Wilde

Old Age

> 66 To me old age is always fifteen years older than I am. 99
>
> **BERNARD BARUCH**

If you want to be adored by your peers and have standing ovations wherever you go—live to be over ninety.

George Abbott

Mr Salteena was an elderly man of 42.

Daisy Ashford

on reaching the age of 100:
If I'd known I was gonna live this long, I'd have taken better care of myself.

Eubie Blake

To what do I attribute my longevity? Bad luck.

Quentin Crisp

You know you're getting old when the candles cost more than the cake.

Bob Hope

20 to 40 is the fillet steak of life. After that it's all short cuts.

Philip Larkin

The thing about getting old is the number of things you think that you can't say aloud because it would be too shocking.

Doris Lessing

I've been around so long, I knew Doris Day before she was a virgin.

Groucho Marx

There's one more terrifying fact about old people: I'm going to be one soon.

P. J. O'Rourke

Growing old is like being increasingly penalized for a crime you haven't committed.

Anthony Powell

How long do you want to wait until you start enjoying life? When you're sixty-five you get social security, not girls.

Neil Simon

The House of Lords is a perfect eventide home.

Baroness Stocks

to a young diplomat who boasted of his ignorance of whist:
What a sad old age you are preparing for yourself.
   Charles-Maurice de Talleyrand

I feel I can talk with more authority, especially when I say,
'I don't know.'
   Peter Ustinov, *on being 80*

Though well stricken in years the old blister becomes on
these occasions as young as he feels, which seems to be
about twenty-two.
   P. G. Wodehouse

Parents

> **In our society...mothers go on getting
> blamed until they're eighty, but shouldn't
> take it personally.**
>   KATHARINE WHITEHORN

My parents and his mother ganged up and had pan-parent
meetings.
   Katy Hayes

Mom and Pop were just a couple of kids when they got married. He was eighteen, she was sixteen, and I was three.

Billie Holiday

If I'm more of an influence to your son as a rapper than you are as a father...you got to look at yourself as a parent.

Ice Cube

to Nina Hamnett:
We have become, Nina, the sort of people our parents warned us about.

Augustus John

Fathers don't curse, they disinherit. Mothers curse.

Irma Kurtz

Because of their size, parents may be difficult to discipline properly.

P. J. O'Rourke

A Jewish man with parents alive is a fifteen-year-old boy, and will remain a fifteen-year-old boy until *they die*!

Philip Roth

I did not throw myself into the struggle for life: I threw my mother into it. I was not a staff to my father's old age: I hung on to his coat tails.

George Bernard Shaw

I wish either my father or my mother, or indeed both of them, as they were in duty both equally bound to it, had minded what they were about when they begot me.

Laurence Sterne

Parties

> You know I hate parties. My idea of hell is a very large party in a cold room, where everybody has to play hockey properly.
>
> **STELLA GIBBONS**

The difficulty about a theatre job is that it interferes with party-going.

Barry Humphries

Unless your life is going well you don't dream of giving a party. Unless you can look in the mirror and see a benign and generous and healthy human being, you shrink from acts of hospitality.

Carol Shields

Gee, what a terrific party. Later on we'll get some fluid and embalm each other.

Neil Simon

An office party is not, as is sometimes supposed, the Managing Director's chance to kiss the tea-girl. It is the tea-girl's chance to kiss the Managing Director.

Katharine Whitehorn

Of course I don't want to go to a cocktail party...If I wanted to stand around with a load of people I don't know eating bits of cold toast I can get caught shoplifting and go to Holloway.

Victoria Wood

Past and Present

66 It's not perfect, but to me on balance Right Now is a lot better than the Good Old Days. 99

MAEVE BINCHY

Nostalgia isn't what it used to be.

Anonymous

The rule is, jam to-morrow and jam yesterday—but never jam today.
Lewis Carroll

They spend their time mostly looking forward to the past.
John Osborne

It used to be a good hotel, but that proves nothing—I used to be a good boy.
Mark Twain

We mustn't prejudge the past.
William Whitelaw

Hindsight is always twenty-twenty.
Billy Wilder

Poetry

> ⁶⁶ Writing a book of poetry is like dropping a rose petal down the Grand Canyon and waiting for the echo. ⁹⁹
>
> **DON MARQUIS**

Poetry is the only art people haven't yet learnt to consume like soup.

W. H. Auden

Sometimes poetry is emotion recollected in a highly emotional state.

Wendy Cope

Immature poets imitate; mature poets steal.

T. S. Eliot

I'd as soon write free verse as play tennis with the net down.

Robert Frost

The notion of expressing sentiments in short lines having similar sounds at their ends seems as remote as mangoes on the moon.

Philip Larkin

My favourite poem is the one that starts 'Thirty days hath September' because it actually tells you something.

Groucho Marx

All that is not prose is verse; and all that is not verse is prose.

Molière

All bad poetry springs from genuine feeling.

Oscar Wilde

Peotry is sissy stuff that rhymes. Weedy people sa la and fie and swoon when they see a bunch of daffodils.

Geoffrey Willans and Ronald Searle

Politics

> 66 He knows nothing; and he thinks he knows everything. That points clearly to a political career. 99
>
> **GEORGE BERNARD SHAW**

Je suis Marxiste—tendance Groucho.

I am a Marxist—of the Groucho tendency.
   Anonymous

Vote for the man who promises least; he'll be the least disappointing.
   Bernard Baruch

The US presidency is a Tudor monarchy plus telephones.
   Anthony Burgess

In politics you must always keep running with the pack. The moment that you falter and they sense that you are injured, the rest will turn on you like wolves.
   R. A. Butler

Politics are almost as exciting as war and quite as dangerous. In war you can only be killed once, but in politics—many times.
   Winston Churchill

There are no true friends in politics. We are all sharks circling, and waiting, for traces of blood to appear in the water.
   Alan Clark

The only safe pleasure for a parliamentarian is a bag of boiled sweets.
   Julian Critchley

Blair goes one way. Brown goes the other way and bang goes the third way.
   Michael Howard

Since when was fastidiousness a quality useful for political advancement?
   Bernard Levin

If voting changed anything they'd abolish it.
   Ken Livingstone

If you want to succeed in politics, you must keep your conscience well under control.
   David Lloyd George

A political culture that has no time for lunch is no culture at all.

Andrew Marr

My New Year resolution is to find where the Labour Party has been buried, and the tomb of the Unknown Socialist.

Austin Mitchell

I'm not going to rearrange the furniture on the deck of the Titanic.

Rogers Morton

Being an MP feeds your vanity and starves your self-respect.

Matthew Parris

Politics is supposed to be the second oldest profession. I have come to realize that it bears a very close resemblance to the first.

Ronald Reagan

An independent is a guy who wants to take the politics out of politics.

Adlai Stevenson

If you want to rise in politics in the United States there is one subject you must stay away from, and that is politics.

Gore Vidal

The Labour Party is going around stirring up apathy.
   William Whitelaw

A liberal is a conservative who's been arrested.
   Tom Wolfe

Poverty

> 66 Poverty is no disgrace to a man, but it is
> confoundedly inconvenient. 99
> **SYDNEY SMITH**

Anyone who has ever struggled with poverty knows how
extremely expensive it is to be poor.
   James Baldwin

Come away; poverty's catching.
   Aphra Behn

It's no disgrace t'be poor, but it might as well be.
   Frank McKinney Hubbard

Everyone was poor and proud. My parents didn't know anything to be proud of, so they just carried on.

Patrick Kavanagh

Look at me. Worked myself up from nothing to a state of extreme poverty.

S. J. Perelman, Will B. Johnstone, and Arthur Sheekman

He was a gentleman who was generally spoken of as having nothing a-year, paid quarterly.

R. S. Surtees

Like dear St Francis of Assisi I am wedded to Poverty: but in my case the marriage is not a success.

Oscar Wilde

Power

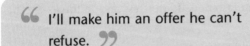

> 66 I'll make him an offer he can't refuse. 99
>
> **MARIO PUZO**

So long as men worship the Caesars and Napoleons, Caesars and Napoleons will duly arise and make them miserable.

   Aldous Huxley

Better to have him inside the tent pissing out, than outside pissing in.

   Lyndon Baines Johnson, *of J. Edgar Hoover*

The Pope! How many divisions has *he* got?

   Joseph Stalin

If you were handed power on a plate you'd be left fighting over the plate.

   Tom Stoppard

He seemed much greater than a private citizen while he still was a private citizen, and by everyone's consent capable of reigning if only he had not reigned.

Tacitus, *of the Emperor Galba*

Children and zip fasteners do not respond to force...Except occasionally.

Katharine Whitehorn

Praise

> 66 I suppose flattery hurts no one, that is, if he doesn't inhale. 99
>
> **ADLAI STEVENSON**

We authors, Ma'am.

Benjamin Disraeli, *to Queen Victoria after the publication of* Leaves from the Journal of our Life in the Highlands *in 1868*

Please don't be too effusive.

Elizabeth II, *adjuration to Tony Blair on the speech he was to make to celebrate her golden wedding*

Consider with yourself what your flattery is worth before
you bestow it so freely.

Samuel Johnson

I used your soap two years ago; since then I have used no
other.

Punch

What really flatters a man is that you think him worth
flattering.

George Bernard Shaw

Among the smaller duties of life, I hardly know one more
important than that of not praising where praise is
not due.

Sydney Smith

Pride

> ❝ His opinion of himself, having once risen, remained at 'set fair'. ❞
>
> **ARNOLD BENNETT**

Modest? My word, no...He was an all-the-lights-on man.
  Henry Reed

But be not afraid of greatness: some men are born great, some achieve greatness, and some have greatness thrust upon them.
  William Shakespeare

I have often wished I had time to cultivate modesty...But I am too busy thinking about myself.
  Edith Sitwell

When I pass my name in such large letters I blush, but at the same time instinctively raise my hat.
  Herbert Beerbohm Tree

Progress

> 66 To you, Baldrick, the Renaissance was just something that happened to other people, wasn't it? 99
>
> **RICHARD CURTIS AND BEN ELTON**

Everywhere one looks, decadence. I saw a bishop with a moustache the other day.

Alan Bennett

All progress is based upon a universal innate desire on the part of every organism to live beyond its income.

Samuel Butler

What have the Romans ever done for us?

John Cleese et al.

Mechanics, not microbes, are the menace to civilization.

Norman Douglas

The civilized man has built a coach, but has lost the use of his feet.

Ralph Waldo Emerson

You can't say civilization don't advance, however, for in every war they kill you in a new way.
   Will Rogers

A swell house with...all the modern inconveniences.
   Mark Twain

Publishing

> 66 If I had been someone not very clever, I would have done an easier job like publishing. 99
>
>   **A. J. AYER**

In a profession where simple accountancy is preferable to a degree in English, illiteracy is not considered to be a great drawback.
   Dominic Behan

The poem will please if it is lively—if it is stupid it will fail—but I will have none of your damned cutting and slashing.
   Lord Byron

Now Barabbas was a publisher.
   Thomas Campbell

A publisher who writes is like a cow in a milk bar.
   Arthur Koestler

I suppose publishers are untrustworthy. They certainly always look it.
   Oscar Wilde

Being published by the Oxford University Press is rather like being married to a duchess: the honour is almost greater than the pleasure.
   G. M. Young

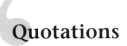

Quotations

> 66 I always have a quotation for everything—
> it saves original thinking. 99
>   DOROTHY L. SAYERS

I know heaps of quotations, so I can always make quite a fair show of knowledge.
   O. Douglas

Next to the originator of a good sentence is the first quoter of it.

Ralph Waldo Emerson

He wrapped himself in quotations—as a beggar would enfold himself in the purple of emperors.

Rudyard Kipling

My favourite quotation is eight pounds ten for a second-hand suit.

Spike Milligan

An anthology is like all the plums and orange peel picked out of a cake.

Walter Raleigh

It seems pointless to be quoted if one isn't going to be quotable...It's better to be quotable than honest.

Tom Stoppard

What a good thing Adam had. When he said a good thing he knew nobody had said it before.

Mark Twain

Religion

66 Things have come to a pretty pass when religion is allowed to invade the sphere of private life. 99

LORD MELBOURNE

Bernard always had a few prayers in the hall and some whiskey afterwards as he was rarther pious but Mr Salteena was not very addicted to prayers so he marched up to bed.
 Daisy Ashford

I've a definite sense of spirituality. I want Brooklyn to be christened, but don't know into what religion yet.
 David Beckham

An atheist is a man who has no invisible means of support.
 John Buchan

I am always most religious upon a sunshiny day.
 Lord Byron

Blessed are the cheesemakers.
 John Cleese et al., *a misheard beatitude*

'Cake or death?' 'Cake, please.'

Eddie Izzard, *imagining how a Church of England Inquisition might have worked*

It's great being a priest, isn't it, Ted?

Graham Linehan and Arthur Mathews

to a clergyman who thanked him for the enjoyment he'd given the world:

And I want to thank you for all the enjoyment you've taken out of it.

Groucho Marx

God is a man, so it must be all rot.

Nancy Nicholson, *just before her marriage to Robert Graves in 1917*

You are not an agnostic...You are just a fat slob who is too lazy to go to Mass.

Conor Cruise O'Brien

He was an embittered atheist (the sort of atheist who does not so much disbelieve in God as personally dislike Him).

George Orwell

People may say what they like about the decay of Christianity; the religious system that produced green Chartreuse can never really die.

Saki

Never take a reference from a clergyman. They always want to give someone a second chance.
  Lady Selborne

Deserves to be preached to death by wild curates.
  Sydney Smith

Protestant women may take the pill. Roman Catholic women must keep taking The Tablet.
  Irene Thomas

Why did the Catholics invent the confessional? What is that but a phone box?
  Peter Ustinov

Royalty

> Everyone likes flattery; and when you come to Royalty you should lay it on with a trowel.
>
> **BENJAMIN DISRAELI**

She is only 5ft 4in, and to make someone that height look regal is difficult. Fortunately she holds herself very well.
Hardy Amies, *of Queen Elizabeth II*

When I appear in public people expect me to neigh, grind my teeth, paw the ground and swish my tail—none of which is easy.
Anne, Princess Royal

King's Moll Reno'd in Wolsey's Home Town.
Anonymous, *US newspaper headline on Wallis Simpson's divorce proceedings in Ipswich*

How different, how very different from the home life of our own dear Queen!
Anonymous, *comment overheard at a performance of Cleopatra by Sarah Bernhardt*

We saw Queen Mary looking like the Jungfrau, white and sparkling in the sun.

Chips Channon

on being asked if Queen Victoria would be happy in heaven:
She will have to walk behind the angels—and she won't like that.

Edward VII

I think everybody really will concede that on this, of all days, I should begin my speech with the words 'My husband and I'.

Elizabeth II, *on her 25th wedding anniversary*

on first seeing Caroline of Brunswick, his future wife:
Harris, I am not well; pray get me a glass of brandy.

George IV

on H. G. Wells's comment on 'an alien and uninspiring court':
I may be uninspiring, but I'll be damned if I'm an alien!

George V

Ah'm sorry your Queen has to pay taxes. She's not a wealthy woman.

John Paul Getty

Another damned, thick, square book! Always scribble, scribble, scribble! Eh! Mr Gibbon?

Duke of Gloucester

I left England when I was four because I found out I could never be King.

Bob Hope

England had declared war on France two weeks after the accession of Queen Anne:

It means I'm growing old when ladies declare war on me.

Louis XIV

My children are not royal, they just happen to have the Queen as their aunt.

Princess Margaret

Really, one might be in Rumania.

Queen Mary, *on the Abdication*

questionnaire for would-be Kings in the Wars of the Roses:

Are you Edmund Mortimer? If not, have you got him?

W. C. Sellar and R. J. Yeatman

He speaks to Me as if I was a public meeting.

Queen Victoria, *of Gladstone*

Science

> It is a good morning exercise for a research scientist to discard a pet hypothesis every day before breakfast.
>
> **KONRAD LORENZ**

When I find myself in the company of scientists, I feel like a shabby curate who has strayed by mistake into a drawing room full of dukes.

W. H. Auden

Basic research is what I am doing when I don't know what I am doing.

Werner von Braun

If an elderly but distinguished scientist says that something is possible he is almost certainly right, but if he says that it is impossible he is very probably wrong.

Arthur C. Clarke

Everybody's a mad scientist, and life is their lab.

David Cronenberg

Equations are more important to me, because politics is for the present, but an equation is something for eternity.

Albert Einstein

Someone told me that each equation I included in the book would halve the sales.

Stephen Hawking

To mistrust science and deny the validity of the scientific method is to resign your job as a human. You'd better go look for work as a plant or wild animal.

P. J. O'Rourke

Science becomes dangerous only when it imagines that it has reached its goal.

George Bernard Shaw

There is something fascinating about science. One gets such wholesale returns of conjecture out of such a trifling investment of fact.

Mark Twain

Secrecy

> A secret in the Oxford sense: you may tell it to only one person at a time.
>
> **OLIVER FRANKS**

The best leaks always take place in the urinal.

John Cole

I know that's a secret, for it's whispered every where.

William Congreve

You might very well think that. I couldn't possibly comment.

Michael Dobbs, *Francis Urquhart's habitual response to questions*

Truth is suppressed, not to protect the country from enemy agents but to protect the Government of the day against the people.

Roy Hattersley

That's another of those irregular verbs, isn't it? I give confidential briefings; you leak; he has been charged under Section 2a of the Official Secrets Act.

Jonathan Lynn and Antony Jay

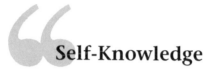

Self-Knowledge

> 66 I'm the girl who lost her reputation and never missed it. 99
>
> **MAE WEST**

Long experience has taught me that to be criticized is not always to be wrong.

Anthony Eden

You'll never have another boss like me, someone who's basically a chilled-out entertainer.

Ricky Gervais and Stephen Merchant, *David Brent welcomes new members of staff*

I'm not a nest-egg person.

Elton John, *giving evidence in court on his average monthly expenditure*

I am not the type who wants to go back to the land; I am the type who wants to go back to the hotel.

Fran Lebowitz

Underneath this flabby exterior is an enormous lack of character.

Oscar Levant

[I am] a doormat in a world of boots.

Jean Rhys

I am extraordinarily patient, provided I get my own way in the end.

Margaret Thatcher

I don't at all like knowing what people say of me behind my back. It makes me far too conceited.

Oscar Wilde

Sex

> A fast word about oral contraception. I asked a girl to go to bed with me and she said 'no'.
>
> **WOODY ALLEN**

On bisexuality: It immediately doubles your chances for a date on Saturday night.
Woody Allen

You should make a point of trying every experience once, excepting incest and folk-dancing.
Anonymous

Give me chastity and continency—but not yet!
St Augustine of Hippo

My mother used to say, Delia, if S-E-X ever rears its ugly head, close your eyes before you see the rest of it.
Alan Ayckbourn

I'll come and make love to you at five o'clock. If I'm late start without me.

Tallulah Bankhead

If homosexuality were the normal way, God would have made Adam and Bruce.

Anita Bryant

He said it was artificial respiration, but now I find I am to have his child.

Anthony Burgess

on homosexuality:
It doesn't matter what you do in the bedroom as long as you don't do it in the street and frighten the horses.

Mrs Patrick Campbell

For flavour, Instant Sex will never supersede the stuff you had to peel and cook.

Quentin Crisp

My dad told me, 'Anything worth having is worth waiting for.' I waited until I was fifteen.

Zsa Zsa Gabor

Sex was a competitive event in those days and the only thing you could take as a certainty was that everyone else was lying, just as you were.

Bob Geldof

Sex is more fun than cars but cars refuel quicker than men.
Germaine Greer

My father told me about the birds and the bees, the liar—I went steady with a woodpecker until I was twenty-one.
Bob Hope

There is no unhappier creature on earth than a fetishist who yearns to embrace a woman's shoe and has to embrace the whole woman.
Karl Kraus

Surely the sex business isn't worth all this damned fuss? I've met only a handful of people who cared a biscuit for it.
T. E. Lawrence, *on reading* Lady Chatterley's Lover

He was into animal husbandry—until they caught him at it.
Tom Lehrer

No sex, please—we're British.
Anthony Marriott and Alistair Foot

Many years ago I chased a woman for almost two years, only to discover that her tastes were exactly like mine: we both were crazy about girls.
Groucho Marx

I always thought music was more important than sex—then I thought if I don't hear a concert for a year-and-a-half it doesn't bother me.
   Jackie Mason

Continental people have sex life; the English have hot-water bottles.
   George Mikes

Not tonight, Josephine.
   Napoleon I

GARY: She put me right on a few technical details, yes.
DERMOT: She said it was like sleeping with a badly-informed labrador.
   Simon Nye

You were born with your legs apart. They'll send you to the grave in a Y-shaped coffin.
   Joe Orton

Your idea of fidelity is not having more than one man in bed at the same time.
   Frederic Raphael

Fancy meeting someone and forgetting you've slept with them. It's not good, is it?
   Arthur Smith

[CHAIRMAN OF MILITARY TRIBUNAL:] What would you do if you saw a German soldier trying to violate your sister? [STRACHEY:] I would try to get between them.

Lytton Strachey

I'm all for bringing back the birch, but only between consenting adults.

Gore Vidal

All this fuss about sleeping together. For physical pleasure I'd sooner go to my dentist any day.

Evelyn Waugh

Why don't you come up sometime, and see me?

Mae West, *usually quoted as, 'Why don't you come up and see me sometime?'*

It's not the men in my life that counts—it's the life in my men.

Mae West

A lot of people are very critical of modern reproductive processes without fully understanding all the ins and outs.

Lord Winston

Singing

> 66 Today if something is not worth saying,
> people sing it. 99
>
> **PIERRE-AUGUSTIN CARON DE BEAUMARCHAIS**

Maybe the most that you can expect from a relationship
that goes bad is to come out of it with a few good songs.
  Marianne Faithfull

Opera is when a guy gets stabbed in the back and, instead
of bleeding, he sings.
  Ed Gardner

Clichés make the best songs. I put down every one I can
find.
  Bob Merrill

The first act of the three occupied two hours. I enjoyed that
in spite of the singing.
  Mark Twain

By the Great Wobbly top note of Jeanette Macdonald!
  Dick Vosburgh

Climb every Mountie.

Dick Vosburgh and Denis King, *rewriting a* Sound of Music
song for Rose Marie

Sleep

> ‟ Sleep is when all the unsorted stuff
> comes flying out as from a dustbin upset
> in a high wind. ”
>
> **WILLIAM GOLDING**

I love sleep because it is both pleasant and safe to use.

Fran Lebowitz

And so to bed.

Samuel Pepys

Men who are unhappy, like men who sleep badly, are
always proud of the fact.

Bertrand Russell

I have had a dream, past the wit of man to say what dream
it was.

William Shakespeare

Many's the long night I've dreamed of cheese—toasted,
mostly.

Robert Louis Stevenson

There ain't no way to find out why a snorer can't hear
himself snore.

Mark Twain

Social Life

> 66 Never speak disrespectfully of Society,
> Algernon. Only people who can't get
> into it do that. 99
>
> **OSCAR WILDE**

I'm a man more dined against than dining.

Maurice Bowra

In London, at the Café de Paris, I sang to café society; in
Las Vegas, at the Desert Inn, I sang to Nescafé society.

Noël Coward

I notice she likes lights and commotion, which goes to show she has social instincts.
Ronald Firbank

Here you are again, older faces and younger clothes.
Mamie Stuyvesant Fish, *habitual greeting to guests*

I do wish we could chat longer, but I'm having an old friend for dinner.
Thomas Harris and Ted Tally , *Hannibal Lecter*

All decent people live beyond their incomes nowadays, and those who aren't respectable live beyond other peoples'.
Saki

Speechmaking

>
>
> When someone asks a question about sex in Hyde Park you double the crowd and halve the argument.
>
> **DONALD SOPER**

I do not object to people looking at their watches when I am speaking. But I strongly object when they start shaking them to make certain they are still going.

Lord Birkett

The most popular speaker is the one who sits down before he stands up.

John Pentland Mahaffy

I speak with more passion on a full bladder.

Enoch Powell

Someone must fill the gap between platitudes and bayonets.

Adlai Stevenson

Whales only get killed when they spout.

Denis Thatcher, *refusing a request for an interview*

Reading a speech with his usual sense of discovery.

Gore Vidal, *of ex-President Eisenhower at the Republican convention of 1964*

Sport

> 66 The thing about sport, any sport, is that swearing is very much part of it. 99
>
> **JIMMY GREAVES**

The trouble with referees is that they just don't care which side wins.

Tom Canterbury

He just can't believe what isn't happening to him.

David Coleman

I love fishing. It's like transcendental meditation with a punch-line.

Billy Connolly

We all get cut and we all get stitched up. We get stud marks down our bodies, we break bones and we lose teeth. We play rugby.
Martin Johnson

I hate all sports as rabidly as a person who likes sports hates common sense.
H. L. Mencken

There's been a colour clash: both teams are wearing white.
John Motson

I can't see who's in the lead but it's either Oxford or Cambridge.
John Snagge

I am here to propose a toast to the sports writers. It's up to you whether you stand or not.
Freddie Trueman

I used to think the only use for it [sport] was to give small boys something else to kick besides me.
Katharine Whitehorn

Jogging is for people who aren't intelligent enough to watch television.
Victoria Wood

Dad's Army kept going in extra time.

Clive Woodward, *on the England team (labelled 'Dad's Army' because of its average age) in the Rugby World Cup final, Sydney, 22 November 2003*

Success

> 66 Whenever a friend succeeds, a little something in me dies. 99
>
> **GORE VIDAL**

to an actor who had lamented, 'I'm failing':

Go on failing. Go on. Only next time, try to fail better.

Samuel Beckett

Success is the one unpardonable sin against our fellows.

Ambrose Bierce

In the end the golden goose will be cooked.

David Blunkett

Where did we go right?

Mel Brooks, *of an unexpected success*

Not for Clan Campbell the loser's mentality that participation is as important as winning.
Alastair Campbell

Whom the gods wish to destroy they first call promising.
Cyril Connolly

If at first you don't succeed, failure may be your style.
Quentin Crisp

The trouble with fulfilling your ambitions is you think you will be transformed into some sort of archangel and you're not. You still have to wash your socks.
Louis de Bernières

I think that's just another word for a washed-up has-been.
Bob Dylan, *on being an 'icon'*

All the rudiments of success in life can be found in ironing a pair of trousers.
Chris Eubank

If at first you don't succeed, try, try again. Then quit. No use being a damn fool about it.
W. C. Fields

My son, the world is your lobster.
Leon Griffiths

Well, we knocked the bastard off!
Edmund Hillary, *on conquering Mount Everest, 1953*

Come forth, Lazarus! And he came fifth and lost the job.
James Joyce

It is sobering to consider that when Mozart was my age he had already been dead for a year.
Tom Lehrer

Success. I don't believe it has any effect on me. For one thing I always expected it.
W. Somerset Maugham

Be nice to people on your way up because you'll meet 'em on your way down.
Wilson Mizner

David Frost has risen without trace.
Kitty Muggeridge

I didn't get where I am today without—.
David Nobbs, *habitual boast of Reggie Perrin's boss CJ*

It is difficult to soar like an eagle when you are surrounded by turkeys.
Helen Osborne, *embroidered on a cushion for John Osborne by his wife*

I never climbed any ladder: I have achieved eminence by sheer gravitation.

George Bernard Shaw

People who reach the top of the tree are only those who haven't got the qualifications to detain them at the bottom.

Peter Ustinov

Moderation is a fatal thing, Lady Hunstanton. Nothing succeeds like excess.

Oscar Wilde

Success is just a matter of luck. Ask any failure!

Earl Wilson

Taxes

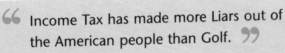

Income Tax has made more Liars out of the American people than Golf.

WILL ROGERS

Tax collectors who'll never know the invigorating joys of treading water in the deep end without a life belt.

Jeffrey Bernard

It was as true...as taxes is. And nothing's truer than them.
   Charles Dickens

The collection of a lunatic and inequitable tax, however
few the victims, must tend to breed an un-English dislike of
taxation in general.
   A. P. Herbert

Logic and taxation are not always the best of friends.
   James C. McReynolds

I'm up to my neck in the real world, every day. Just you try
doing your VAT return with a head full of goblins.
   Terry Pratchett

What is the difference between a taxidermist and a tax
collector? The taxidermist takes only your skin.
   Mark Twain

Technology

 The first rule of intelligent tinkering is to save all the parts.

PAUL RALPH EHRLICH

When man wanted to make a machine that would walk he created the wheel, which does not resemble a leg.

Guillaume Apollinaire

Inanimate objects are classified scientifically into three major categories—those that don't work, those that break down, and those that get lost.

Russell Baker

Let's be frank, the Italians' technological contribution to humankind stopped with the pizza oven.

Bill Bryson

Electric typewriters keep going 'mmmmmmm—what are you waiting for?'

Anthony Burgess

For a successful technology, reality must take precedence over public relations, for nature cannot be fooled.
  Richard Phillips Feynman

Technology...the knack of so arranging the world that we need not experience it.
  Max Frisch

The itemised phone bill ranks up there with suspender belts, Sky Sports Channels and Loaded magazine as inventions women could do without.
  Maeve Haran

The thing with high-tech is that you always end up using scissors.
  David Hockney

Take up car maintenance and find the class is full of other thirty-something women like me, looking for a fella.
  Marian Keyes

Dr Strabismus (Whom God Preserve) of Utrecht has patented a new invention. It is an illuminated trouser-clip for bicyclists who are using main roads at night.
  J. B. Morton

The photographer is like the cod which produces a million eggs in order that one may reach maturity.
  George Bernard Shaw

JACKIE: (*very slowly*) Take Tube A and apply to Bracket D.
VICTORIA: Reading it slower does not make it any easier to do.

Victoria Wood

Television

> *Television*? The word is half Greek, half Latin. No good can come of it.
>
> C. P. SCOTT

TV—a clever contraction derived from the words Terrible Vaudeville...we call it a medium because nothing's well done.

Goodman Ace

Adams' first law of television: the weight of the backside is greater than the force of the intellect.

Phillip Adams

Television is more interesting than people. If it were not, we should have people standing in the corners of our rooms.

Alan Coren

Television is for appearing on, not looking at.

Noël Coward

I don't watch television, I think it destroys the art of talking about oneself.

Stephen Fry

Being taken no notice of in 10 million homes.

David Hare, *of appearing on television*

It's television, you see. If you are not on the thing every week, the public think you are either dead or deported.

Frankie Howerd

Television is simultaneously blamed, often by the same people, for worsening the world and for being powerless to change it.

Clive James

My show is the stupidest show on TV. If you are watching it, get a life.

Jerry Springer

It always makes me laugh when people ask why anyone would want to do a sitcom in America. If it runs five years, you never have to work again.

Twiggy

Never miss a chance to have sex or appear on television.
   Gore Vidal

It used to be that we in films were the lowest form of art.
Now we have something to look down on.
   Billy Wilder

Tennis

> 66 No one is more sensitive about his game
> than a weekend tennis player. 99
>   JIMMY CANNON

I call tennis the McDonald's of sport—you go in, they make
a quick buck out of you, and you're out.
   Pat Cash

New Yorkers love it when you spill your guts out there. Spill
your guts at Wimbledon and they make you stop and clean
it up.
   Jimmy Connors

I WISH *I'D* SAID THAT   195

Someone in the locker room said my matches should come with a health warning.

Tim Henman

You cannot be serious!

John McEnroe, *to a Wimbledon umpire*

All gong and no dinner...we just wish Anna would finally win something aside from hearts.

Tim Sheridan, *of the Russian tennis star Anna Kournikova at Wimbledon 2000*

The Theatre

66 God, send me some good actors. Cheap. 99

LILIAN BAYLIS

STUDENT: Did Hamlet actually have an affair with Ophelia?
ACTOR-MANAGER: In our company, always.

Anonymous

*on being asked 'What was the message of your play' after a
performance of The Hostage:*
Message? Message? What the hell do you think I am, a
bloody postman?
 Brendan Behan

A play wot I wrote.
 Eddie Braben, *spoken by Ernie Wise*

after a play about Napoleon had failed:
Never, never, will I do another play where a guy writes with
a feather.
 Max Gordon

If any play has been produced only twice in three hundred
years, there must be some good reason for it.
 Rupert Hart-Davis

I understand your play is full of single entendre.
 George S. Kaufman, *to Howard Dietz on* Beat the Devil

Satire is what closes Saturday night.
 George S. Kaufman

I didn't like the play, but then I saw it under adverse
conditions—the curtain was up.
 Groucho Marx

Don't clap too hard—it's a very old building.
John Osborne

House Beautiful is play lousy.
Dorothy Parker

You don't expect me to know what to say about a play
when I don't know who the author is, do you?
George Bernard Shaw

It's pure theatrical Viagra.
Charles Spencer, *on* The Blue Room, *starring Nicole Kidman*

In the old days, you went from ingenue to old bag, with a
long stretch of unemployment in between.
Julie Walters

When you think about it, what other playwrights are there
besides O'Neill, Tennessee and me?
Mae West

The play was a great success, but the audience was a total
failure.
Oscar Wilde

Thought

> 66 My brain? It's my second favourite
> organ. 99
> **WOODY ALLEN AND MARSHALL BRICKMAN**

I have tried too in my time to be a philosopher; but, I don't know how, cheerfulness was always breaking in.
   Oliver Edwards

Apart from the known and the unknown, what else is there?
   Harold Pinter

Sometimes I sits and thinks, and then again I just sits.
   Punch

What a waste it is to lose one's mind, or not to have a mind. How true that is.
   Dan Quayle

There are also unknown unknowns—the ones we don't know we don't know.
   Donald Rumsfeld

What is your aim in philosophy?—To show the fly the way out of the fly-bottle.

Ludwig Wittgenstein

You would not enjoy Nietzsche, sir. He is fundamentally unsound.

P. G. Wodehouse

Time

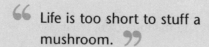

> 66 Life is too short to stuff a mushroom. 99
>
> SHIRLEY CONRAN

on receiving an invitation for 9 a.m.:
Oh, are there two nine o'clocks in the day?

Tallulah Bankhead

arriving at Dublin Castle for the handover by British forces on 16 January 1922, and being told that he was seven minutes late:
We've been waiting 700 years, you can have the seven minutes.

Michael Collins

There was a pause—just long enough for an angel to pass, flying slowly.
   Ronald Firbank

I'll be with you in the squeezing of a lemon.
   Oliver Goldsmith

We have passed a lot of water since then.
   Sam Goldwyn

Time spent on any item of the agenda will be in inverse proportion to the sum involved.
   C. Northcote Parkinson

Eternity's a terrible thought. I mean, where's it all going to end?
   Tom Stoppard

[Treason], Sire, is a question of dates.
   Charles-Maurice de Talleyrand

Transport

> 66 The only way of catching a train I ever discovered is to miss the train before. 99
>
> **G. K. CHESTERTON**

parking problems:
That's OK, we can walk to the kerb from here.
Woody Allen

Railways and the Church have their critics, but both are the best ways of getting a man to his ultimate destination.
Revd W. Awdry

In America there are two classes of travel—first class, and with children.
Robert Benchley

'Glorious, stirring sight!' murmured Toad, never offering to move. 'The poetry of motion! The *real* way to travel! The *only* way to travel!...O poop-poop! O my! O my!'
Kenneth Grahame

Cyclists see motorists as tyrannical and uncaring. Motorists believe cyclists are afflicted by a perversion.
　　Boris Johnson

I feel about airplanes the way I feel about diets. It seems to me that they are wonderful things for other people to go on.
　　Jean Kerr

'Take my camel, dear,' said my aunt Dot, as she climbed down from this animal on her return from High Mass.
　　Rose Macaulay

seeing the Morris Minor prototype in 1945:
It looks like a poached egg—we can't make that.
　　Lord Nuffield

What is better than presence of mind in a railway accident? Absence of body.
　　Punch

Walk! Not bloody likely. I am going in a taxi.
　　George Bernard Shaw

BOATMAN: I 'ad that Christopher Marlowe in the back of my boat.
　　Tom Stoppard

Anybody seen in a bus over the age of 30 has been a failure in life.

Loelia, Duchess of Westminster

Travel

> ❝ It is not worthwhile to go around the world to count the cats in Zanzibar. ❞
>
> **HENRY DAVID THOREAU**

They say travel broadens the mind; but you must have the mind.

G. K. Chesterton

A person can be stranded and get by...two people with a German shepherd and no money are in a mess.

Andrea Dworkin

At my age travel broadens the behind.

Stephen Fry

Abroad is bloody.

George VI

on the Giant's Causeway:
Worth seeing, yes; but not worth going to see.
   Samuel Johnson

What good is speed if the brain has oozed out on the way?
   Karl Kraus

Thanks to the interstate highway system, it is now possible
to travel from coast to coast without seeing anything.
   Charles Kuralt

Everybody in fifteenth-century Spain was wrong about
where China was and as a result, Columbus discovered
Caribbean vacations.
   P. J. O'Rourke

If it's Tuesday, this must be Belgium.
   David Shaw

Truth

> **The truth is rarely pure, and never simple.**
>
> **OSCAR WILDE**

Our old friend...economical with the *actualité*.
  Alan Clark

Something unpleasant is coming when men are anxious to tell the truth.
  Benjamin Disraeli

It is always the best policy to speak the truth—unless, of course, you are an exceptionally good liar.
  Jerome K. Jerome

Never tell a story because it is true: tell it because it is a good story.
  John Pentland Mahaffy

The presence of those seeking the truth is infinitely to be preferred to those who think they've found it.
  Terry Pratchett

I never give them [the public] hell. I just tell the truth, and they think it is hell.

Harry S. Truman

There was things which he stretched, but mainly he told the truth.

Mark Twain

Virtue

> ❝ The louder he talked of his honour, the faster we counted our spoons. ❞
>
> **RALPH WALDO EMERSON**

I'm as pure as the driven slush.

Tallulah Bankhead

Lydia was tired of being good…It made her feel a little dowdy, as though she had taken up residence in the suburbs of morality.

Alice Thomas Ellis

But if he does really think that there is no distinction
between virtue and vice, why, Sir, when he leaves our
houses, let us count our spoons.
Samuel Johnson

He that but looketh on a plate of ham and eggs to lust after
it, hath already committed breakfast with it in his heart.
C. S. Lewis

I think I could be a good woman if I had five thousand a
year.
William Makepeace Thackeray, *Becky Sharp*

When I'm good, I'm very, very good, but when I'm bad,
I'm better.
Mae West

I've been things and seen places.
Mae West

I used to be Snow White...but I drifted.
Mae West

Between two evils, I always pick the one I never tried
before.
Mae West

I can resist everything except temptation.

Oscar Wilde

A little sincerity is a dangerous thing, and a great deal of it is absolutely fatal.

Oscar Wilde

War

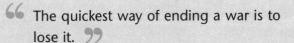

66 The quickest way of ending a war is to lose it. 99

GEORGE ORWELL

of the retreat from Dunkirk, May 1940:
The noise, my dear! And the people!

Anonymous

After each war there is a little less democracy to save.

Brooks Atkinson

A war hasn't been fought this badly since Olaf the Hairy, high chief of all the Vikings, ordered 80,000 battle helmets with the horns on the inside.

Richard Curtis and Ben Elton, *Blackadder's comment*

I'd like to see the government get out of war altogether and leave the whole field to private industry.
    Joseph Heller

TRENTINO (Louis Calhern): I am willing to do anything to prevent this war.
FIREFLY (Groucho Marx): It's too late. I've already paid a month's rent on the battlefield.
    Bert Kalmar et al.

Gentlemen, you can't fight in here. This is the war room.
    Stanley Kubrick , Terry Southern, and Peter George

The first step in having any successful war is getting people to fight it.
    Fran Lebowitz

Like many men of my generation, I had an opportunity to give war a chance, and I promptly chickened out.
    P. J. O'Rourke

Evelyn Waugh, returning from Crete in 1941, was asked his impression of his first battle:
Like German opera, too long and too loud.
    Evelyn Waugh

As Lord Chesterfield said of the generals of his day, 'I only hope that when the enemy reads the list of their names, he trembles as I do.'
Duke of Wellington

'Anything in the papers, Jeeves?' 'Some slight friction threatening in the Balkans, sir.'
P. G. Wodehouse

There is only one way for a young man to get on in the army. He must try and get killed in every way he possibly can!
Garnet Wolseley

 Wealth

> 66 I've been poor and I've been rich—rich is better. 99
>
> **SOPHIE TUCKER**

It was a sumpshous spot all done up in gold with plenty of looking glasses.
Daisy Ashford

If you would know what the Lord God thinks of money, you have only to look at those to whom he gives it.
  Maurice Baring

People say I wasted my money. I say 90 per cent went on women, fast cars and booze. The rest I wasted.
  George Best

When I hear a rich man described as a colourful character I figure he's a bum with money.
  Jimmy Cannon

The Rich aren't like us—they pay less taxes.
  Peter de Vries

£40,000 a year [is] a moderate income—such a one as a man might jog on with.
  Lord Durham

A rich man is nothing but a poor man with money.
  W. C. Fields

To trust people is a luxury in which only the wealthy can indulge; the poor cannot afford it.
  E. M. Forster

The meek shall inherit the earth, but not the mineral
rights.
  John Paul Getty

I am a Millionaire. That is my religion.
  George Bernard Shaw

It is the wretchedness of being rich that you have to live
with rich people.
  Logan Pearsall Smith

It was very prettily said, that we may learn the little value
of fortune by the persons on whom heaven is pleased to
bestow it.
  Richard Steele

I sometimes wished he would realize that he was poor
instead of being that most nerve-racking of phenomena, a
rich man without money.
  Peter Ustinov

The Weather

> It was such a lovely day I thought it was a pity to get up.
>
> **W. SOMERSET MAUGHAM**

on being asked why he never sunbathed in California instead of sitting under a sun-lamp:
And get hit by a meteor?
Robert Benchley

Summer has set in with its usual severity.
Samuel Taylor Coleridge

It ain't a fit night out for man or beast.
W. C. Fields

Some are weather-wise, some are otherwise.
Benjamin Franklin

I said, 'It is most extraordinary weather for this time of year.' He replied, 'Ah, it isn't this time of year at all.'
Oliver St John Gogarty

The most serious charge which can be brought against New England is not Puritanism but February.

Joseph Wood Krutch

The rain drove us into the church...Limerick gained a reputation for piety, but we knew it was only the rain.

Frank McCourt

I have a horror of sunsets, they're so romantic, so operatic.

Marcel Proust

Come December, people always say, 'Isn't it cold?' Well, of course it's cold. It's the middle of winter. You don't wander around at midnight saying, 'Isn't it dark?'

Arthur Smith

Thank heavens, the sun has gone in, and I don't have to go out and enjoy it.

Logan Pearsall Smith

Let no man boast himself that he has got through the perils of winter till at least the seventh of May.

Anthony Trollope

The way to ensure summer in England is to have it framed and glazed in a comfortable room.

Horace Walpole

It was the wrong kind of snow.
Terry Worrall, *explaining disruption on British Rail*

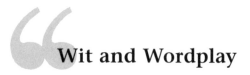

Wit and Wordplay

> 'Curiouser and curiouser!' cried Alice.
>
> **LEWIS CARROLL**

You've got to take the bull between your teeth.
Sam Goldwyn

I can answer you in two words, im-possible.
Sam Goldwyn

'*Succès d'estime*' translates as 'a success that ran out of steam'.
George S. Kaufman

The greatest thing since they reinvented unsliced bread.
William Keegan

Epigram: a wisecrack that played Carnegie Hall.
Oscar Levant

What's a geriatric? A German footballer scoring three goals?
Bob Monkhouse

Comparisons are odorous.
William Shakespeare

He is the very pineapple of politeness!
Richard Brinsley Sheridan

If I reprehend any thing in this world, it is the use of my
oracular tongue, and a nice derangement of epitaphs!
Richard Brinsley Sheridan

No caparisons, Miss, if you please!—Caparisons don't
become a young woman.
Richard Brinsley Sheridan

She's as headstrong as an allegory on the banks of the Nile.
Richard Brinsley Sheridan

on seeing Mrs Grote in a huge rose-coloured turban:
Now I know the meaning of the word 'grotesque'.
Sydney Smith

You will find as you grow older that the weight of rages will press harder and harder upon the employer.
    William Archibald Spooner

You have tasted your worm, you have hissed my mystery lectures, and you must leave by the first town drain.
    William Archibald Spooner, *to an undergraduate*

I'm aghast! If there ever was one.
    Dick Vosburgh

I'm on the horns of a Dalai Lama.
    Dick Vosburgh

OSCAR WILDE: How I wish I had said that.
WHISTLER: You will, Oscar, you will.
    James McNeill Whistler

Women

> 66 It was a blonde. A blonde to make a bishop kick a hole in a stained glass window. 99
>
> **RAYMOND CHANDLER**

Zuleika, on a desert island, would have spent most of her time in looking for a man's footprint.

Max Beerbohm

The suffragettes were triumphant. Woman's place was in the gaol.

Caryl Brahms and S. J. Simon

I heard a man say that brigands demand your money *or* your life, whereas women require both.

Samuel Butler

When a woman isn't beautiful, people always say, 'You have lovely eyes, you have lovely hair.'

Anton Chekhov

I'd have opened a knitting shop in Carlisle and been a part of life.

Quentin Crisp, *on his regret at not being born female*

'O! help me, heaven,' she prayed, 'to be decorative and to do right!'

Ronald Firbank

I didn't fight to get women out from behind the vacuum cleaner to get them onto the board of Hoover.

Germaine Greer

She who must be obeyed.

Rider Haggard

A woman's preaching is like a dog's walking on his hinder legs. It is not done well; but you are surprised to find it done at all.

Samuel Johnson

Remember, you're fighting for this woman's honour...which is probably more than she ever did.

Bert Kalmar et al.

Women do not find it difficult nowadays to behave like men, but they often find it extremely difficult to behave like gentlemen.

Compton Mackenzie

When women kiss it always reminds one of prize-fighters shaking hands.
   H. L. Mencken

The thinking man's crumpet.
   Frank Muir, *of Joan Bakewell*

I'd the upbringing a nun would envy...Until I was fifteen I was more familiar with Africa than my own body.
   Joe Orton

That woman speaks eighteen languages, and can't say No in any of them.
   Dorothy Parker

I do see her in tough joints more than somewhat.
   Damon Runyon

A woman without a man is like a fish without a bicycle.
   Gloria Steinem

We are becoming the men we wanted to marry.
   Gloria Steinem

There are worse occupations in this world than feeling a woman's pulse.
   Laurence Sterne

I blame the women's movement for 10 years in a boiler suit.

Jill Tweedie

Many a woman has a past, but I am told that she has at least a dozen, and that they all fit.

Oscar Wilde

Words

> 66 In my youth there were words you couldn't say in front of a girl; now you can't say 'girl'. 99
>
> **TOM LEHRER**

Acronyms are your allies. They sound impressive while conveying no information. Use them liberally.

Scott Adams

Serendipity means searching for a needle in a haystack and instead finding a farmer's daughter.

Anonymous

You see it's like a portmanteau—there are two meanings packed up into one word.

Lewis Carroll

It depends on what the meaning of 'is' is.

Bill Clinton, *videotaped evidence to the grand jury; tapes broadcast 21 September 1998*

Two such wonderful phrases—'I understand perfectly' and 'That is a lie'—a précis of life, aren't they?

Brian Friel

Some word that teems with hidden meaning—like Basingstoke.

W. S. Gilbert

They say the definition of ambivalence is watching your mother-in-law drive over a cliff in your new Cadillac.

David Mamet

He respects Owl, because you can't help respecting anybody who can spell TUESDAY, even if he doesn't spell it right.

A. A. Milne

Déshabillé. It meant untidy, but with bags and bags of style.

Terry Pratchett

Make me a beautiful word for doing things tomorrow; for that surely is a great and blessed invention.
  George Bernard Shaw

I asked my teacher what an oxymoron was and he said, 'I don't know what an "oxy" is, bastard.'
  Arthur Smith and Chris England

In modern life nothing produces such an effect as a good platitude. It makes the whole world kin.
  Oscar Wilde

Work

66 I do nothing, granted. But I see the hours pass—which is better than trying to fill them. 99

  E. M. CIORAN

A professional is a man who can do his job when he doesn't feel like it. An amateur is a man who can't do his job when he does feel like it.
  James Agate

If you want to get to know someone better, you shouldn't take them out for a candlelit dinner, you should watch them at work. When they're full of concentration, only not concentrating on you.
   Julian Barnes

If I am doing nothing, I like to be doing nothing to some purpose. That is what leisure means.
   Alan Bennett

I suspect guys who say, 'I just send out for a sandwich for lunch,' as lazy men trying to impress me.
   Jimmy Cannon

I never work. Work does age you so.
   Quentin Crisp

I was proud to work with the great Gershwin, and I would have done it for nothing, which I did.
   Howard Dietz

I have long been of the opinion that if work were such a splendid thing the rich would have kept more of it for themselves.
   Bruce Grocott

It is impossible to enjoy idling thoroughly unless one has plenty of work to do.
   Jerome K. Jerome

Work expands so as to fill the time available for its completion.

C. Northcote Parkinson

It's true hard work never killed anybody, but I figure why take the chance?

Ronald Reagan

I understand. You work very hard two days a week and you need a five-day weekend. That's normal.

Neil Simon

Always suspect any job men willingly vacate for women.

Jill Tweedie

Work is the curse of the drinking classes.

Oscar Wilde

Writers

> 66 I love being a writer. What I can't stand is the paperwork. 99
>
> **PETER DE VRIES**

I am someone who's permanently pregnant with a play.
Alan Ayckbourn

Authors with a mortgage never get writer's block.
Mavis Cheek

An author who speaks about his own books is almost as bad as a mother who talks about her own children.
Benjamin Disraeli

It is splendid to be a great writer, to put men into the frying pan of your words and make them pop like chestnuts.
Gustave Flaubert

The defendant, Mr. Haddock, is, among other things, an author, which fact should alone dispose you in the plaintiff's favour.

A. P. Herbert

Tell them the author giveth and the author taketh away.

George S. Kaufman, *to a playwright afraid to tell the cast of cuts he had made*

We writers all act and react on one another; and when I see a good thing in another man's book I react on it at once.

Stephen Leacock

There is no need for the writer to eat a whole sheep to be able to tell you what mutton tastes like. It is enough if he eats a cutlet. But he should do that.

W. Somerset Maugham

I am the kind of writer that people think other people are reading.

V. S. Naipaul

The shelf life of the modern hardback writer is somewhere between the milk and the yoghurt.

Calvin Trillin

To see him [Stephen Spender] fumbling with our rich and delicate language is to experience all the horror of seeing a Sèvres vase in the hands of a chimpanzee.

Evelyn Waugh

Let Shakespeare do it his way, I'll do it mine. We'll see who comes out better.

Mae West

I know no person so perfectly disagreeable and even dangerous as an author.

William IV

Writing

> 66 No man but a blockhead ever wrote, except for money. 99
>
> **SAMUEL JOHNSON**

If you can't annoy somebody with what you write, I think there's little point in writing.

Kingsley Amis

The biggest obstacle to professional writing is the necessity for changing a typewriter ribbon.
  Robert Benchley

The only thing that goes missing in Nature is a pencil.
  Robert Benchley

Let alone re-write, he doesn't even re-read.
  Clive James

If you want to get rich from writing, write the sort of thing that's read by persons who move their lips when reading.
  Don Marquis

If you steal from one author, it's plagiarism; if you steal from many, it's research.
  Wilson Mizner

As to the Adjective: when in doubt, strike it out.
  Mark Twain

Anyone could write a novel given six weeks, pen, paper, and no telephone or wife.
  Evelyn Waugh

I don't give a toss about writing really. It's a bit ironic that the things I'm really into are music and football, and I have never really been good at either.

Irvine Welsh

Youth

> **It is better to waste one's youth than to do nothing with it at all.**
>
> **GEORGES COURTELINE**

Remember that as a teenager you are at the last stage in your life when you will be happy to hear that the phone is for you.

Fran Lebowitz

If you had seen me in my teens you would have bolted for the door without picking up your coat.

Joanna Lumley

Youth is wasted on the young. I'm 52 now and I just can't stay up all night like I did.

Camille Paglia

It's all that the young can do for the old, to shock them and keep them up to date.

George Bernard Shaw

What music is more enchanting than the voices of young people, when you can't hear what they say?

Logan Pearsall Smith

Give me a girl at an impressionable age, and she is mine for life.

Muriel Spark

One's prime is elusive. You little girls, when you grow up, must be on the alert to recognize your prime at whatever time of your life it may occur.

Muriel Spark

Being young is not having any money; being young is not minding not having any money.

Katharine Whitehorn